Run The Rockies

Classic Trail Runs in Colorado's Front Range

Steven Bragg

The Colorado Mountain Club Press
Golden, Colorado

Published by The Colorado Mountain Club Press. Founded in 1912, the Colorado Mountain Club is the largest outdoor recreation, education and conservation organization in the Rocky Mountains. Look for our books at your favorite book seller or contact us at:

    710 10th Street, Suite 200, Golden, CO 80401,
    Phone: (303) 996-2743, Email address: *cmcpress@cmc.org*,
    Website: *http://www.cmc.org*

Managing Editor for CMC Press: Gretchen Hanisch.
Graphics Design and Maps: Terry Root, Gretchen Hanisch, Mike
                            Jackson, Eric Starck, Andrew Terrill,
                            and Lyn Berry
Proofing: Gretchen Hanisch and Terry Root
Front cover photo: Ruuner at Boulder Mountain Park,
    © Omni Photo Communications, Inc./Index Stock Imagery
Except as credited, all other photographs by Steven Bragg
Text copyright 2004: © Steven Bragg

Run the Rockies
  by Steven Bragg
  Library of Congress Control Number: 2004000041
  ISBN # 0-9724413-5-2

We gratefully acknowledge the financial support of the people of Colorado, through the Scientific and Cultural Facilities District of greater metropolitan Denver, for our publishing activities.

Printed in Canada

The
Colorado
Mountain
Club's
CMC CLASSICS series

of guidebooks explores the very best of the Colorado Rockies as only the CMC can. With nearly a century of experience, leading thousands of outings a year into the backcountry, we've earned the title *experts in the Rockies*. Discover new wonders, hike or ski a classic route, scale a famous fourteener — we'll lead you there with these authoritative guides. Income from sales helps to support our mission of conservation and outdoor education.

Classics
This symbol indicates trips that have become CMC Classics — favorites of the Colorado Mountain Club, enjoyed year-after-year. We recommend these trips because of their outstanding scenic or wilderness qualities — or because they are just, plain fun!

Classics

Colorado's best from the experts in the Rockies

Meet The Author

Steve Bragg is a two-time President of the Colorado Mountain Club, as well as its Treasurer for five years. He has climbed over 500 peaks on six continents, including more than 350 peaks exceeding an elevation of 13,000 feet and all 54 of Colorado's 14,000-foot peaks. He has climbed five of the continental high points, as well as 46 of the 50 state high points. He has also mountain biked the 470-mile Colorado Trail in both directions - solo. He is also an expert alpine skier and a certified Rescue Diver.

Steve has been the Chief Financial Officer or controller of four companies, as well as a consulting manager at Ernst & Young and auditor at Deloitte & Touche. He received a master's degree in finance from Bentley College, an MBA from Babson College, and a bachelor's degree in economics from the University of Maine. He is also one of the most prolific business authors in the United States, having published 17 accounting books.

Author's Dedication

To Lee Kinney of The Custom Foot, who rescued my knees with great custom insoles.

Table of Contents

Introduction to Runs in the Colorado Springs Area   157

THE RUNS   SPECIAL CONSIDERATIONS (see page 10)   PAGE

Appendix 180

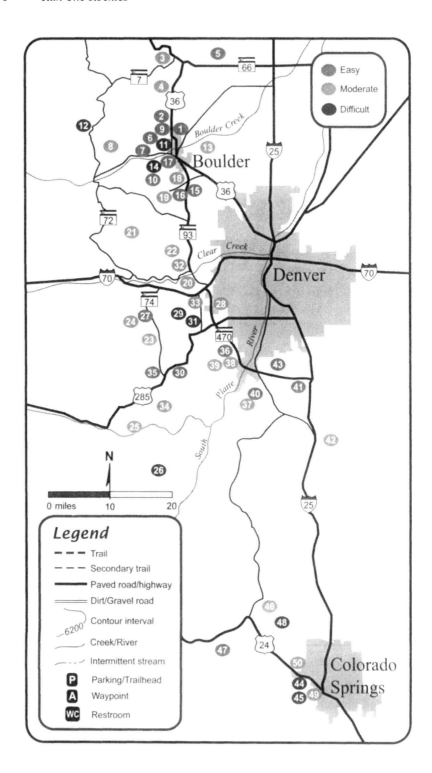

The Joys of Trail Running

Like many of you, I began running while in school as part of the track team. The standard routine was to pound along a paved road for miles, while breathing in the fumes of cars racing by a few feet away. After a few years, it became more difficult to rouse myself for these workouts, especially when I underwent a knee surgery at age 20, and then had a knee lock up again a few years later - essentially ending any competitive racing aspirations.

Years later, I saw runners cruising along the trails that I was hiking, carrying nothing more than a water bottle and a small fanny pack. Fascinated, I tried it myself and loved it at once. Strangely enough, I could run for miles without any knee problems, because the dirt surface was so much more forgiving than the rock-hard asphalt of my youth. Also, the constant changes of pace to avoid rocks and roots appears to be better for my body, while also making runs far more interesting. Best of all, the great sights and smells of the Front Range are stunning - hot air balloons rising over local reservoirs, early morning fog in the valleys, rushing streams, and the smell of pine trees in the early morning as the sun filters through their branches.

The variety of these trails is enormous. They range from the placid smoothness of the Doudy Draw Trail to the fiendish steepness and jagged rocks of Mount Sanitas, just a few miles away from each other in Boulder. Further south along the Front Range, one can run in the vastly social atmosphere of the superbly maintained Barr Trail on the side of Pikes Peak, or back off a few miles and run the pleasant 14-mile loop trail around Rampart Reservoir, with great views of Pikes Peak.

An unusual side benefit of trail running is that runners are looked upon as the gods of the trail. Hikers frequently cannot believe that someone is running past them, miles from the nearest road, and not only will stand aside, but will do so with a grin and sometimes even a cheer of encouragement.

For all the runs in this book, the amount of mileage involving pavement is kept to the absolute minimum - less than one mile in total, and most of that on one unavoidable segment of the excellent Rampart Reservoir Loop. I have found that, once you try trail running, not only will you not go back to road running, but you may find yourself avoiding it at all costs.

How To Use This Guide

Trail descriptions are arranged in north-to-south order, with Boulder area runs listed near the beginning and Colorado Springs area runs near the end. I have diverged from the difficulty rating promulgated by the Colorado Mountain Club (CMC) in a number of instances if the circumstances make a run more or less difficult than the CMC's rating system. Look for these rating symbols that appear with each run:

Easy: *Up to 4.5 miles and up to 1,000 feet vertical gain.*   ***Moderate***: *4.6 to 7.9 miles and up to 2,000 feet vertical gain.*   ***Difficult***: *8.0+ miles and over 2,000 feet vertical gain.*

Information Blocks

Each trail run in this book includes an *information block* listing essential facts about each run. Use this information to quickly tell whether this run is right for you and your abilities.

Location indicates the general trailhead location, so that you may pick a run in an area that may be convenient for you or in an area that interests you.

Distance/Type indicates the round trip mileage for the route and the type of run, whether it be an *out-and-back* route, a *loop* or a *medley* of trails. An *out-and-back* trail generally retraces its steps (although it may include a short loop.) A *loop* is a complete clockwise or counter-clockwise circuit, with minimal duplication of any trail segments. (Although loops can be run in either direction, a preferred direction is indicated in the detailed route descriptions, as well as by arrows on the trail maps.) Finally, a *medley* combines many trails and (more importantly) many trail junctions, which will likely require you to bring this book along as a reference guide.

An estimated **Running Time** is noted, which generally corresponds to about five miles per hour, or four miles per hour if the trail is exceptionally steep. Please adjust these time estimates to your own pace.

Starting Elevation and **Elevation Gain** are self explanatory. But the latter is especially important, in conjunction with the provided Elevation Profile of each run, in assessing the energy required for an outing. The calculation of elevation gain includes the increases in elevation for all changes in the trail, not just the difference between the beginning elevation and the highest point along the trail.

Best Season refers to the optimum time of the year to enjoy a particular route. Certain trails at higher elevations or on north-facing slopes may have significant snow and ice cover for a portion of the year that would discourage all but the most hardcore of runners. However, the majority of routes described here in the sunny Front Range can be enjoyed nearly year-round.

If you have questions about specific rules and regulations or have suggestions about managing the public lands that these routes traverse, you may contact the land management agencies listed under **Jurisdiction**. You'll find the contact addresses for these agencies in the Appendix. In particular, be sure to contact Mueller State Park about trail closures during the elk calving season, which is usually in June.

Listed under **Map(s)** are relevant maps that cover the described route. Those from *Trails Illustrated* (readily available at most outdoor retailers) are preferred, as they are weather-proof, tear-resistant and generally more up-to-date than the familiar USGS 7 1/2' minute "topos". State parks and several county and city parks often have kiosks at or near major trailheads with brochures/maps that are suitable for navigating the routes in this guide. Maps issued by the Forest Service are fine for driving to the trailhead, but lack enough detail to be of use on the trail.

Park **permit/fee** requirements are also listed, which mostly applies to state parks such as Castlewood Canyon, Roxborough and Eldorado Canyon. Fees are generally collected at self-serve kiosks where bill changing is not available.

Next, each trail is also **graded**. This is a description of the trail surface to be encountered, as well as (in some cases) an average angle of ascent or a beginner, intermediate, or difficult rating. Special hazards are also noted.

The **Getting There** section contains a detailed description of how to find the trailhead. Most access descriptions begin at a major highway exit or intersection. For instance, many of the Boulder area descriptions begin at the intersection of Canyon Boulevard and 28th Street, which is a convenient central point for the city. It is useful to have a good road map on hand while studying the descriptions. Under normal conditions, all of the trailheads in this guide can be reached by a regular passenger car (no four-wheel drive required).

Since many runners will find it impractical to carry this guide book on every run, we also provide a short, encapsulated description of each route that you can quickly jot down on a piece of paper. Look for these *GO* **Boxes** before you hit the trail!

Trail Map and Elevation Profile

Each trail run in this book is accompanied by a **Trail Map** and **Elevation Profile** to help you find your way. The maps describe terrain in terms of 200 foot contour intervals shown by the colored lines. At a glance, close lines indicate steeper terrain. You'll find a legend explaining the symbols used on these maps on page 6. This guide is *GPS Enabled*, providing you with a chart of selected waypoints in Latitude/Longitude. When used with map datum NAD 27, these coordinates provide an approximate location fix (normally, no more than 15 meters off in the case of most hand-held GPS units.)

The Route Description

The **Route Description** describes the entire route in detail, including the mile marker at which trail junctions arise, and the elevation at that point, rounded to the nearest ten feet.

Also, the Appendix lists the addresses and phone numbers of the various park districts in which the trails are located, as well as contains a list of the more popular trail races in Colorado, sorted by month.

Please read the following sections on trail running mechanics, clothing and navigation before perusing the list of trails, so you will be better prepared when you venture off the paved path. Even if you have lived in the region for many years and feel that you already know that information, be sure to read the **Dangers on the Trail** section, which lists specific trails on which certain dangers, such as West Nile Virus and lightening, are more likely.

Special Considerations: Look for these special symbols next to runs in the *Table of Contents*, to help you choose a run that is right for you:

Dog Runs: If you like to run with your canine companion, or if you wish to avoid trails where dogs may be present, look for this symbol. Dogs MUST be leashed (except some trails in the City of Boulder Open Space and Mountain Parks system.)

Bicyclists: This symbol indicates runs popular with bicyclists. Pedestrians (runners and hikers) always have right-of-way. However, be alert for oncoming bikes at all times, especially on blind curves. You may choose to avoid these trails on busy weekends.

Lightening: Short but violent afternoon thunderstorms are a frequent occurrence along Colorado's Front Range in the summer. You may choose to do runs indicated by this symbol early in the day before potentially dangerous storms build up.

Fall Runs: Running in autumn in Colorado is especially pleasant with ideal temperatures, little chance of afternoon storms, and colorful displays of quaking aspen and scrub oak. This symbol indicates some runs that are perfect in September and October.

Some of these trail runs have become **CMC Classics** — favorites of the Colorado Mountain Club, that are enjoyed year-after-year. We highly recommend these trips because of their outstanding scenic or wilderness qualities — or because they are just plain fun! Look for this symbol next to the trail run descriptions.

The Mechanics of Running

Trail running is entirely different from pounding the pavement through the local neighborhood. Trails can be vastly more difficult to negotiate, while there are also stream crossings, snow banks, roots, and rocks to navigate. Here are a few pointers on altering your running technique to match the great outdoors:

Downhill Running

It sure is fun to blast down a root-infested trail, but you'll end up in the hospital if you do it for long. Instead, cut the length of your stride in order to retain control, and try to hop over trail obstructions instead of landing on them.

Uphill Running

There are plenty of steep uphill stretches on the Front Range! Though switching into a power walk is a reasonable option, consider continuing in a running posture, but taking very small steps. Alternatively, this is a great time to slow down and use the moment to eat and drink while waiting for your pulse to drop back down out of the danger category.

Ice

There is a reason why mountain climbers attach crampons to their boots when they climb ice - it is dangerous. If you see ice, slow down to a shuffle. If there is a steep run-out below the ice, consider the risk of slipping down it. This is a good way to be seriously injured. Ice is not a joke.

Running at Lair O' the Bear Park in winter. (Gretchen Hanisch)

Snow

The north-facing sides of many Front Range trails are buried in snow long after their south-facing counterparts have dried out. When you reach such places, don't necessarily turn around - snow can be quite fun if there are only a few inches of it, since it covers rocks and roots, sometimes making the run easier. The real problem is route finding, especially if there are no trail markers or footprints. If so, it is better to turn around than to proceed and risk getting lost.

Sand and Gravel

There are short stretches of sand and gravel on many Colorado trails. Shorten your stride and slow down in these sections. It is quite easy to accumulate a quarry-full of gravel in your running shoes in short order, so be sure to lace your shoes up to the very top in order to present the smallest possible opening through which it can enter.

Stream Crossings

Do not remove your shoes, since it is very difficult to feel the stream bottom in the intensely cold water of the Front Range. Also, use a stick as support and to feel your way across the stream. If the stream is too deep or the water is rushing by with considerable speed, turn around and go home. In Colorado, stream crossings drown people every year.

Water Bars

A water bar is either a wooden beam or a ¼" thick strip of rubber placed across the trail. The Jefferson County Open Space trail maintenance staff appears particularly fond of these devices. It is quite easy to trip over them, so either practice high-stepping to avoid them, or time your steps so that the bars are in the middle of each stride.

Vision

Trail running requires the same vision technique used for bump skiing. Focus primarily on the area directly in front of you in order to spot and avoid projections in the trail, but also regularly glance ahead perhaps ten to twenty yards in order to see what is coming, and to plot the easiest course.

In general, slow down. Way down. It is extremely easy to stub a toe on any of the myriad of projections poking out of a trail, so keep your speed down and pay close attention to where you are placing your feet. High speed sprints are rarely safe on a trail run. On the harder trails, you should be prepared for many walking segments, and should not be embarrassed when it happens. Further, it is useful to consciously relax your upper body when negotiating difficult trails; by doing so, your body tends not to lean so far back, thereby improving your balance.

~~othi~~ng, Food and Hydration

Though it is possible to occasionally see someone miles from the nearest trailhead, running in the skimpiest clothing and carrying nothing else, trail running normally requires somewhat more equipment and preparation than the standard neighborhood jog. Some of the longer trail runs in this book can place you miles from the nearest trailhead, so think about preparing for adverse weather and other problems with the following tips.

Clothing

Though most runners bound through the Front Range in just their usual road running clothes, there are a few extra considerations that may alter your clothing choice. First, the Front Range is at a higher elevation, so the sun's rays are more intense. For that reason, this is a good place to wear a sun hat with a protective fringe, as well as a long-sleeve shirt. Second, many of the trails noted in this guide contain roots, rocks and other nefarious items that may trip you and send you sprawling. If so, wearing long sleeves and long pants (usually tights) will provide a bit more protection from scrapes.

During the colder months, wearing a head band or hat, as well as gloves or mittens, should be mandatory. Hats containing the *Windstopper* fabric are especially good at blocking the wind. A number of extremely light-weight shell jackets are also available, typically weighing no more than six ounces. The only problem with these jackets is the elimination of such features as underarm zippers, pockets, and wrist closures in order to reduce weight.

Though most of the trails listed in this book do not require expedition-level stream crossings, it is still possible to get wet feet. If so, use wool-blend socks, so you have some slight chance of remaining comfortable in wet shoes. Finally, consider buying socks in a color other than white, since they won't retain that color more than ten minutes into a muddy trail run.

Shoes

Skimpy road racing shoes do not work well on trails. Instead, look for beefy tread that give you the maximum grip on loose trail surfaces. Also, look for a wide strip of rubber over the toe area (a toe bumper) to give some protection when you inevitably stub a toe on a rock or root. For extra toe protection, get a shoe with extra room in the toe area so your feet have room to slide forward during steep descents. Further, be sure to purchase shoes with a wide base, so there is less chance of a painful ankle roll. In addition, consider purchasing a custom insole that will give not only more support but also better protection than the typically low-quality standard insoles found in most shoes. Finally, buy new shoes every 500 miles or so, because a shoe's midsole, which provides all the cushioning, will have begun to collapse by that time.

A key issue is the type of material used in the top part of the shoe. If it contains a large amount of plastic or leather to improve durability, it is also likely to breathe less and feel hot after a number of miles. Also, this type of shoe is difficult to dry out once it becomes wet. Accordingly, many runners opt for a lighter mesh fabric that breaths better and allows the shoe to dry out faster.

Food

You may find your energy flagging after an hour of laboring up a tough incline. Carrying a few cereal bars is an excellent way to maintain a steady energy level for the duration of a run. A particularly effective solution is the carbohydrate energy gel, which comes in small squeegee tubes. These gels contain about an ounce of high-concentration carbohydrate solution, and should be taken about every forty minutes during a run. Unfortunately, they are very expensive, costing at least $1/ounce.

Hydration

The Front Range is such a dry climate that you can lose water at an astounding rate. Even a run only lasting an hour can result in a pound of water loss. Most of the runs in this book are designed to last between one and three hours, so you will need to bring some form of hydration with you. Many runners bring a hand-held 12-ounce bottle with them and secure it to a hand with a neoprene strap, though more popular hydration units involve the use of a backpack containing a water bladder or a waist belt holding one or more smaller water bottles. The author's favorite is a low-profile backpack containing a 70-ounce water bladder.

A water bladder is not a good place to store an energy drink, since it is extremely difficult to clean the drinking tube. If you find it necessary to use an energy drink during a run, carry water in the bladder and store the energy drink in a separate bottle that is easier to clean.

In case you run out of water and need to obtain water from a pond or stream, consider bringing a small bottle of iodine tablets. Add one tablet to each quart of water, and wait 30 minutes for it to kill the bacteria in the water. Be sure to replace the tablets as of the recommended

Running in full sun on a hot day increases your hydration requirements.

date listed on the bottle. For added safety, obtain water from a running source, such as a stream, rather than still water, since the volume of harmful bacteria tends to be less in running water. The primary reason for these preventive measures is giardia, which causes significant short-term abdominal cramping and diarrhea.

Once a run is complete, don't stop drinking! It can take several hours to fully re-hydrate after an especially long or hot run. This is a good time to drink a quart or more of an energy drink

Dangers On The Trail

Though trail running keeps you away from those noisy and smelly automobiles, it can also put you uncomfortably in touch with the more dangerous side of nature. This section addresses some of the more hazardous aspects of trail running, and how to deal with them.

Bears

Yes, there are bears in Colorado, and lots of them. Documented bear attacks are quite rare, though if you do enough trail running, your odds of spotting a bear in the wild are reasonably good. The theory on how to handle bears seems to change from year to year, but generally states that you should make yourself appear as small and inconsequential as possible, at which point the bear will not feel threatened, and will lumber off. Also, absolutely never get between a bear cub and its parent. Be sure to read any warnings posted at trailheads regarding the proper way to treat bears in the wild.

The author has now had five bear encounters. In all cases, the bears were just as startled as I was, and both parties sprinted away in opposite directions, thereby rendering the above advice unworkable. I have taken to making as much noise as possible prior to approaching areas where bears might be located, such as thickets or blind spots in the trail, on the theory that they will be adequately warned of my approach and will go away. Some runners even attach small bells to their shoelaces in order to create a built-in early warning system for bears.

Lightening

Enormous thunderstorms build up along the Front Range, spawning extraordinary lightening displays that present the greatest risk to runners of all the dangers presented here. The best way to avoid lightening is to run as early as possible in the day, before thunderstorms have a chance to form. This means being off the trails by noon at the latest. Also, some of the trails described here have scant nearby vegetation, making you the tallest object out there, and therefore the likeliest target for a lightening strike. The following trails are particularly barren, leaving you open to more risk of a lightening strike:

Boulder Area
Community Ditch Trail
Doudy Draw Trail

Eagle/Sage Loop
Foothills Trail Extension
Hogback Loop
Rabbit Mountain
Teller Farm Trails

Denver Area
Bluffs Park Loop
Green Mountain Loop

Mountain Lions

Though quite rare, mountain lions have been spotted in all of the trail running areas covered by this book. In 1991, an 18 year-old runner was killed by a mountain lion near Idaho Springs, which falls just to the west of the region in this book - in short, the danger is real. Current theory states that you should make yourself look as large as possible, speak in a soothing voice, and back away slowly from a mountain lion. They are also more likely to attack someone running away from them, so walk away instead. This is only the current view of how to defend yourself against a mountain lion, so be sure to read any warnings posted at trailheads regarding this issue.

Rattlesnakes

Yes, rattlesnakes do reside along the Front Range, but you are unlikely to encounter one unless you step off trail, and even then only on some of the lower elevation trails. If you see one, give it a wide berth and continue on your way. A snake can strike an object a distance of half its body length, and more so if striking downhill, so stay at least twice that far away. The author has seen rattlesnakes sunning themselves in the parking lot at Roxborough Park in Denver, and near the side of the Mesa Trail

Rattlesnake warning at Blufs Park

in Boulder. The Bluffs Park in south residential Denver even posts rattlesnake warning signs. Nonetheless, a prolific runner may never see
one.

West Nile Virus

The most recent scourge to reach the Front Range is the mosquito-
borne West Nile Virus. Though one can contract it pretty much anywhere in the running areas described in this book, there are a few ways
to at least reduce the risk of contracting it. First, apply a layer of mosquito repellent containing a high proportion of DEET. However, be
mindful that some people have adverse reactions to DEET. Also, runners can sweat off a DEET application at a prodigious rate, so bring a
small container along on a run and be prepared to make multiple appli-
cations. Also, do not apply it near the eyes or mouth, and certainly not
near any open cuts or scrapes.

Second, avoid running at dawn or dusk, when mosquitoes are out
in the greatest concentrations. Third, avoid those trail runs where are
higher concentrations of mosquitoes, typically due to standing water or
marshy conditions near the trail. The following trails are more subject
to mosquito incursions:

Boulder Area
Anne U. White Trail
Eagle/Sage Loop
Enchanted Mesa Medley
Teller Farm Trails

Denver Area
Castlewood Canyon Loop
High Line Canal Trail

Running Alone

Running alone is a wonderfully peaceful experience, but can also
be fatal. Both human and animal predators are much more likely to
attack a single person. This is a particular problem in trail running,
where there is sufficient masking foliage in many places to easily hide
a predator. If you cannot find another person to run with, at least limit
your runs to daylight hours when other people are more likely to be
present. Also, consider running with a small air horn (available at sport-
ing goods shops for boaters), which can scare off predators, or a small
can of mace. Since an attack can come at any time, having a preventive
or offensive weapon tucked away in your pack will not be of much use.
Instead, keep it on a short tether and loop the tether over your hand.

Running alone can present risks.

Human predators are certainly an issue. In 2003, a female trail runner was kidnapped from the popular Highline Canal Trail at dusk and repeatedly raped. The rapist was reported to have used a stun gun in the assault. Though one may dream about suddenly producing a large-caliber weapon to drastically shorten the lifespan of such people, the fact remains that trail runners run light, and have minimal room for protective equipment. Consequently, plan runs in a preventive manner, carry the defensive items just noted, and use the trail runner's natural advantage - run away as fast as you can.

A final note: if you escape an attack of any kind, report it to the authorities immediately, so preventive measures can be taken to keep anyone else from being injured or killed.

Navigation

Despite the generally high quality of trail signs on the Front Range, it is still possible to get lost. Trail runners generally don't like to haul a trail guide along with them, much less a compass, altimeter, or GPS unit. A reasonable alternative is to purchase one of the new multi-purpose wrist watches that combine the standard timekeeping function with an altimeter and compass. One manufacturer has even released a watch that includes a GPS function, though it is quite bulky. Whatever else you may choose to leave behind, bring a map!

If you become lost, take out the map and plot the elevation on your wrist altimeter against your last known elevation, which typically reduces the range of your possible locations to a very small area. Be aware that altimeters tend to show a slightly lower reading than your actual elevation as the altitude increases. For example, the altimeter can read 13,500 feet when you are standing on top of a 14,000 foot peak, so adjust accordingly. Next, use your wrist compass feature to determine the direction in which the trail should be heading in your vicinity, and move in that direction until you find the trail. If you are on a hillside, a simple approach is to use the map to determine the elevation of the trail, then use the altimeter to find your elevation, and then move uphill or downhill until your elevation matches that of the trail.

I highly recommend using a GPS unit for the more complex trail descriptions. Each trail in this book includes a table of waypoints for all major trail junctions, which you can load into a GPS unit, along with

*Checking the map
(courtesy Colorado Mountain Club)*

a topographical base map, and carry with you in one hand as you navigate a route. A high-end GPS unit has the added benefit of showing your exact elevation and compass bearing. The main problem with GPS units is their penchant for chewing up batteries - expect to replace the batteries every eight hours. It may be worthwhile to bring a spare set of batteries with you on a run.

Finally, for those who like to run late in the day or evening, strongly consider purchasing a small handheld flashlight or, better yet, an ultralight headlamp. There have been dramatic improvements in headlamp technology in the last few years, resulting in extraordinarily tiny headlamps with combinations of LED and conventional bulbs.

Wilderness Responsibilities

The outings in this guide traverse a number of publicly managed land units, including National Forests, Colorado State Park lands and several parks under local control by counties or cities. Please be cognizant of the fact that private land often abuts these units. Respect any private property and "no trespassing" postings. Remember also that federal law protects cultural and historic sites on public lands, such as old cabins, mines and Indian sites. These historic, cultural assets are important to us all as a society, and are not meant to be scavenged for personal gain.

Forest Service occupancy regulations are primarily designed to limit wear and tear in fragile wilderness areas. However, even non-wilderness areas need to be treated lightly to preserve resources for future generations. Strive to leave no trace of your passing and follow the principles of **Leave No Trace**.

The Leave No Trace Message promotes and inspires responsible outdoor recreation through education, research, and partnerships. Managed as a non-profit educational organization, authorized by the Forest Service, LNT is about enjoying places like the Colorado Rockies, while traveling and camping with care.

Before starting your outing check with the Forest Service

Leave No Trace

The seven LNT Principles of outdoor ethics form the framework of LNT's message:

1. *Plan Ahead and Prepare*
2. *Travel and Camp on Durable Surfaces*
3. *Dispose of Waste Properly*
4. *Leave What You Find*
5. *Minimize Campfire Impacts*
6. *Respect Wildlife*
7. *Be Considerate of Other Visitors*

Leave No Trace, Inc.
P.O. Box 997
Boulder, CO 80306
(800) 332-4100
(303) 442-8217 Fax
www.lnt.org

for the current forest fire danger, which can sometimes be extreme, and for any restrictions on campfires. A list of contact addresses for Forest Service offices, and the offices of other publicly managed lands is provided on page 181.

Boulder Area

In alphabetical order, the trails itemized in this section are as follows:

Boulder North

Eagle/Sage Loop
Foothills Trail Extension
Hall Ranch Loop
Heil Ranch
Rabbit Mountain

Boulder Central and West

Anne U. White Trail
Betasso Preserve Loop
Glacier Lake Road
Hogback Loop
Meyers Homestead Trail
Mount Sanitas / Dakota Ridge
Sourdough Trail
Teller Farm Trails
Walker Ranch Loop

Boulder South

Community Ditch Trail
Doudy Draw Trail
Enchanted Mesa Medley
Mesa Trail Loop
Rattlesnake Gulch Trail

Boulder's Flatirons are in view on the Enchanted Mesa Medley.

Boulder is the outdoor recreation capital of Colorado. Within a few minutes drive of downtown Boulder, one can go rock climbing, mountain biking, kayaking, gliding, and hot air ballooning - not to mention trail running. The city is dominated by the Flatirons, a stunning range of upthrust peaks containing some of the finest rock climbing in the state, including such legendary climbs as The Maiden, the Third Flatiron, and of course all of Eldorado Canyon, where climbers begin their ascents directly from the access road. The unwary runner may also be buzzed by low-flying gliders along the crest of the Flatirons.

All this activity is fueled by thousands of residents of the University of Colorado at Boulder, who infest the foothills on weekends and between classes. Some occasionally even attend classes! The University's buildings are nestled in a broad valley over which preside the tan buildings of the National Center for Atmospheric Research (NCAR), which are perched atop a hill just to the south of town.

Unfortunately, being in a valley, the city is also subject to some pollution, so expect a brown cloud over the area when colder winter air slides down from the mountains and traps hotter polluted air rising from the city.

Activities are centered along four roads. To the south, Eldorado Springs Drive leads from Route 93 to Eldorado Canyon State Park. Along the way, one can stop at parking areas for access to the Community Ditch, Doudy Draw, and Mesa Trails. Further north, Flagstaff Road ascends Flagstaff Mountain, passing the famous Flagstaff House restaurant (offering a sweeping view of Boulder), and continuing to parking areas for the Homestead Trail and Walker Ranch. Heading west from downtown Boulder, Boulder Canyon Road (Route 119) takes one alongside the heavily-used Boulder Creek Path and several rock climbing areas, past Betasso Preserve, and eventually to Barker Reservoir and Nederland. Finally, Route 36 continues north out of Boulder towards the Heil Valley Ranch and Hall Ranch running areas; dozens of road cyclists use this road as a training route all the way north to Lyons and beyond.

The only problem with Boulder is its traffic system. There are several photo speed traps along Route 36 that will automatically fine you for speeding, while a maze of traffic lights can reduce a catatonic monk to a frenzy within a few miles. Though a healthy dose of sedatives will resolve the issue, the basic problem is that too many people find Boulder to be the most perfect spot on earth, and have demonstrated their enthusiasm by living there.

The quality of trail maintenance varies widely in the Boulder region, with the best trails invariably being designated as "hiker only." A good example is the Hall Ranch Loop, well to the north of Boulder, which features the exquisite "hiker only" Nighthawk Trail on the outbound segment and several much more eroded "general purpose" trails on the return leg. Some trails are seriously in need of maintenance, such as the Sourdough, Mount Sanitas, and Walker Ranch trail systems. Nonetheless, when the Boulder Parks and Recreation staff is determined to create a high-quality trail, the result is first class. Examples are the Enchanted Mesa Medley and Mesa Trail Loop. Clearly the finest concentration of trails is located just to the east of the Flatirons, to the south of Boulder. Everyone else has figured this out too, so expect to see lots of other runners in the same region. Strangely, the difficult Mount Sanitas sees a fair number of runners, either because this is a macho pursuit or it is so close to downtown. Another area popular with runners is the Eagle/Sage Loop just to the north of town and the Teller Farm Trails, located just to the east.

Be forewarned that many of the trails in the Boulder Parks and Recreation system are dog-friendly. Runners and hikers may recreate, with their pooches off-leash, as long as they maintain "voice and sight" control. In practice, this works fine for everyone most of the time. However, the tons of dog waste created each year has been identified as a problem. If you like to run with your canine companion, you'll enjoy Boulder's excellent trail system; but please pick up after your dog. If you would rather avoid trails with high numbers of dogs, avoid certain trails on busy weekends; especially Mesa Trail Loop, Enchanted Mesa Medley, Community Ditch Trail and Doudy Draw Trail.

Eagle/Sage Loop 1

Running by pond at the junction of Eagle Trail and Sage Trail.

*T*his trail run is an excellent opportunity to explore the beautiful wetlands areas around the Mesa Reservoir, which provide a lush habitat for an array of water and grassland birds.

Rating

Easy

Location: Just outside the Boulder city limits on its northern fringe.

Distance/Type: 5.6 miles loop

Running Time: 1.0 hour

Starting Elevation: 5,545 feet

Elevation Gain: 360 feet

Best Season: Nearly year-round, although quite exposed to weather.

Jurisdiction: City of Boulder Open Space & Mtn. Parks (Boulder Valley Ranch)

Map(s): *Trails Illustrated #100*

Permits/Fees: None

Grade: Exceptionally easy. Most of the route is on wide double track, with the exception of some narrower trails near the beginning and end of the route.

Getting There: From the corner of 28th Street and Canyon Boulevard in Boulder, drive north on 28th Street for 4.0 miles until Route 7 merges in on the left. Then take the next dirt road on the right, a matter of an extra hundred yards, and drive 0.2 miles to the Foothills Trailhead parking area on the left side of the road.

Mileage

0.0 Start east out of the parking lot.

0.2 Bear east on Degge Trail.

1.1 Go east on Mesa Reservoir Loop.

1.3 Turn east on Eagle Trail.

2.8 Go west on Sage Trail.

4.0 Bear west onto Cobalt Trail.

4.9 Join Hidden Valley Trail. Go south.

5.2 Turn west on Degge Trail.

5.6 Arrive at the trailhead.

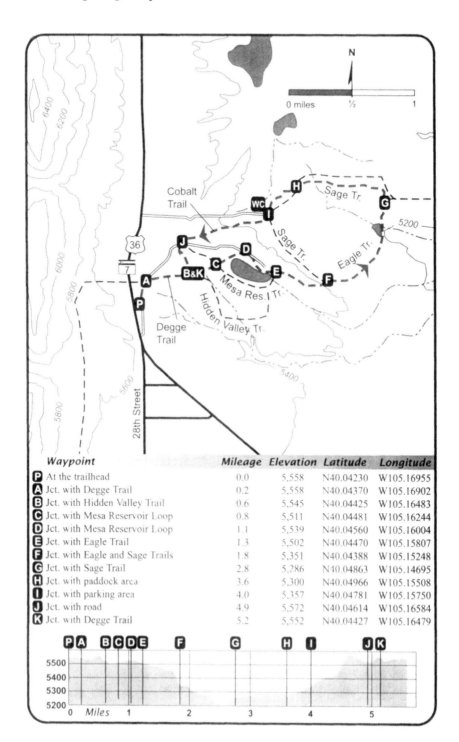

Waypoint		Mileage	Elevation	Latitude	Longitude
P	At the trailhead	0.0	5,558	N40.04230	W105.16955
A	Jct. with Degge Trail	0.2	5,558	N40.04370	W105.16902
B	Jct. with Hidden Valley Trail	0.6	5,545	N40.04425	W105.16483
C	Jct. with Mesa Reservoir Loop	0.8	5,511	N40.04481	W105.16244
D	Jct. with Mesa Reservoir Loop	1.1	5,539	N40.04560	W105.16004
E	Jct. with Eagle Trail	1.3	5,502	N40.04470	W105.15807
F	Jct. with Eagle and Sage Trails	1.8	5,351	N40.04388	W105.15248
G	Jct. with Sage Trail	2.8	5,286	N40.04863	W105.14695
H	Jct. with paddock area	3.6	5,300	N40.04966	W105.15508
I	Jct. with parking area	4.0	5,357	N40.04781	W105.15750
J	Jct. with road	4.9	5,572	N40.04614	W105.16584
K	Jct. with Degge Trail	5.2	5,552	N40.04427	W105.16479

The Route Description

Run out of the east end of the parking area and turn right onto the dirt road you used to access the parking lot. Follow it for 100 yards and turn right at a road junction. Continue another 100 yards to where the road turns sharply right, and pass through a gate at the corner, bringing you to a trail junction at mile 0.2 (5560). Take the Degge Trail, which heads due east through open plains and up over a low hill to a trail junction at mile 0.6 (5550), where there is a four-way junction with the Hidden Valley Trail. Continue straight ahead on the Degge Trail. Do the same at mile 0.8, where the trail crosses the Mesa Reservoir Loop. Shortly thereafter, the trail passes to the left of the exquisite Mesa Reservoir, site of a significant wetlands area.

The trail then curls away from the reservoir and merges with the Mesa Reservoir Loop at mile 1.1 (5540) onto which you will take a right turn. A key junction is at mile 1.3 (5500), site of a metal awning, where you depart the Mesa Reservoir Loop and turn left through a gate to access the Eagle Trail. This takes you out over an exposed butte (don't run it in stormy weather!) and down a moderately steep headwall to a junction with the Sage and Eagle Trails at mile 1.8 (5350). Turn right to stay on the Eagle Trail.

You now embark on a wide loop of a combination wetlands and grazing area, heading east, then north, and then back west to encircle most of the area. After passing a beautiful pond on the eastern end of the route, you will travel north up a short hill and then turn left at mile 2.8 (5290) to access the Sage Trail. Follow the Sage Trail through mile 3.9 (5300), where a side trail branches off to the left, passing by a paddock area. Stay with the main Sage Trail, passing through a gate 100 yards later and continuing through a cow pasture, eventually reaching a parking area at mile 4.0 (5360), where you can make use of the bathroom facilities. Then pass the bathrooms and turn right onto the Cobalt Trail, which heads east through open plains until you reach a road crossing at mile 4.9 (5570). Cross the road and take the Hidden Valley Trail on its other side, which takes you back to the Degge Trail at mile 5.2 (5550). Turn right onto the Degge Trail and follow it back to the parking area, which you will reach at mile 5.6 (5560).

2 Foothills Trail Extension

This route provides an ideal introduction to trail run-ning due to its ease and its rel-atively short distance. This is the perfect run for a beautiful Boulder morning due to its lack of tree cover. And because of its proximity to the Hogback Loop route at the same trailhead, it can be prolonged for a little extra mileage when your in the mood.

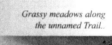

Grassy meadows along the unnamed Trail.

Rating

Easy

GO

Mileage

0.0 Start west on Foothills Trail.
0.5 Turn north on an unnamed trail.
2.3 Turn around retracing path.
4.1 Rejoin Foothills Trail. Go East.
4.6 Arrive at the trail-head.

Location: Just outside the Boulder city limits on its northern fringe.
Distance/Type: 4.6 miles out and back
Running Time: 45 minutes
Starting Elevation: 5,545 feet
Elevation Gain: 200 feet
Best Season: Nearly year-round
Jurisdiction: City of Boulder Open Space & Mtn. Parks
Map(s): *Trails Illustrated # 100*
Permits/Fees: None

Grade: An extremely easy grade on firm soil, with few rocks. The only downside is a rather narrow trail, so wear long running tights if the grass is wet.

Getting There: From the corner of 28th Street and Canyon Boulevard in Boulder, drive north on 28th Street for 4.0 miles until Route 7 merges in on the left. Then take the next dirt road on the right, a mat-ter of an extra hundred yards, and drive 0.2 miles to the Foothills Trailhead parking area on the left side of the road.

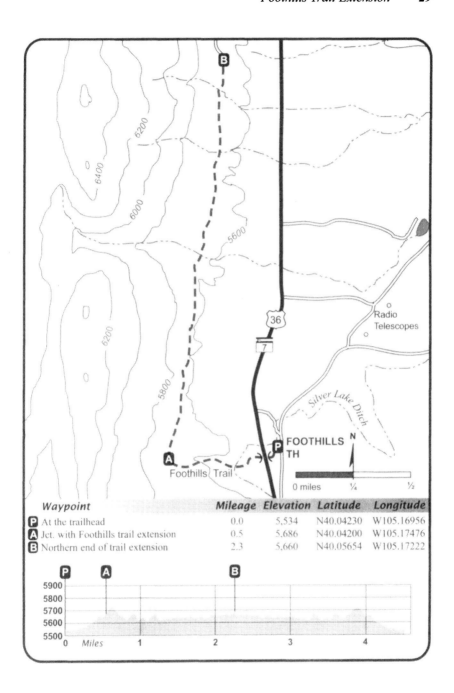

Waypoint	Mileage	Elevation	Latitude	Longitude
P At the trailhead	0.0	5,534	N40.04230	W105.16956
A Jct. with Foothills trail extension	0.5	5,686	N40.04200	W105.17476
B Northern end of trail extension	2.3	5,660	N40.05654	W105.17222

The Route Description

Take the Foothills Trail west out of the parking lot and run through the tunnel underneath Route 36. Continue until mile 0.5 (5690), where you leave the Foothills Trail just before a rusted gate and turn sharply north onto an unnamed trail. If the Foothills Trail starts going steeply uphill, you have gone too far.

The trail is extremely flat, proceeding north about a ½ mile to the west of Route 36. Ignore all trails branching off to either side, of which there are several small ones. When in doubt, head straight north. You will come to a dead end at a chain link fence at mile 2.3 (5660), which is marked "No Trespassing." Turn around and run back to the car, which you will reach at mile 4.6 (5530).

Hall Ranch Loop 3

Running along the Nighthawk Trail..

It does not get any better than the first half of this route, which is on the Nighthawk Trail - really one of the finest runs in the Colorado Front Range, especially near its western end where spectacular views of Longs Peak appear.

Rating

Moderate

Classics

Location: 17.0 miles north of Boulder
Distance/ Type: 9.5 miles loop
Running Time: 2.0 hours
Starting Elevation: 5,455 feet
Elevation Gain: 1,550 feet
Best Season: Spring into Fall
Jurisdiction: Boulder County Parks & Open Space (Hall Ranch)
Map(s): Trails Illustrated #100
Permits/Fees: None

Grade: An average six degree angle of ascent seems easy on the excellent Nighthawk Trail. The route becomes more rocky and uncertain during its second half, primarily on the Bitterbrush Trail, which is somewhat more eroded.

Getting There: From the intersection of 28th Street and Canyon Boulevard in Boulder, drive north on Route 36 for 14.2 miles to the intersection with Route 66. Turn left to stay on Route 36 and stay on it for 1.5 miles until you reach a junction with Route 7. Turn left to travel southbound on Route 7, and follow it for 1.4 miles until the parking area for Hall Ranch appears on the right.

Mileage

0.0 Start west of out of the parking lot.
0.2 Bear west onto the Nighthawk Trail.
3.8 Continue west on Nighthawk Trail.
4.7 Turn north onto Nelson Loop Trail.
5.9 Go North onto Bitterbrush Trail.
7.3 Bear south onto Bitterbrush Trail.
9.5 Arrive at the parking lot.

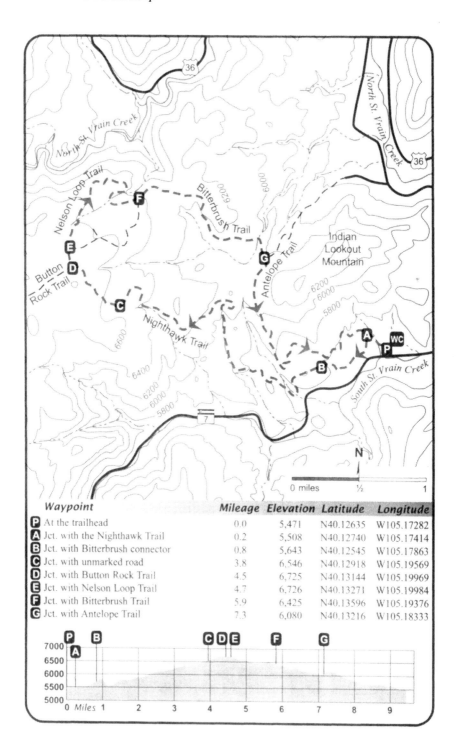

Waypoint	Mileage	Elevation	Latitude	Longitude
P At the trailhead	0.0	5,471	N40.12635	W105.17282
A Jct. with the Nighthawk Trail	0.2	5,508	N40.12740	W105.17414
B Jct. with Bitterbrush connector	0.8	5,643	N40.12545	W105.17863
C Jct. with unmarked road	3.8	6,546	N40.12918	W105.19569
D Jct. with Button Rock Trail	4.5	6,725	N40.13144	W105.19969
E Jct. with Nelson Loop Trail	4.7	6,726	N40.13271	W105.19984
F Jct. with Bitterbrush Trail	5.9	6,425	N40.13596	W105.19376
G Jct. with Antelope Trail	7.3	6,080	N40.13216	W105.18333

The Route Description

The route is designed in a clockwise manner, and is strongly recommended in that sequence, since you then have the option to turn around at the far western end of the route and return on the Nighthawk Trail, rather than completing the loop on the much busier Bitterbrush Trail, which is open to a horde of mountain bikers.

There is a parking next to the road, as well as a higher one at the end of a short access road. These instructions assume you are starting at the less-crowded lot next to the road. From that point, take the trail beginning at the west end of the parking lot. Turn left onto the Nighthawk Trail at mile 0.2 (5510). Follow the trail through open meadows, ignoring a connector trail to the Bitterbrush Trail branching off to the right at mile 0.8 (5640). The trail gradually ascends as it rolls through a mix of meadows and scattered trees, generally (unfortunately) staying within hearing range of Route 7 to the south. A confusing point is at mile 3.8 (6550), just to the left of a small rock formation, where the trail appears to split. Stay on the better-defined single track trail that veers to the left, ignoring a less well-defined double track trail curling away to the north.

The run becomes entirely worthwhile at mile 4.5 (6730), where you enter a meadow with fabulous views of Longs Peak to the west. The Button Rock Trail also departs to the left here. Ignore it and continue on the Nighthawk Trail to mile 4.7 (6730), where you turn left onto the Nelson Loop Trail. This is a multi-use trail that allows mountain bikers, so expect considerably more traffic from this point on. If you prefer a quieter descent, turn around and return on the Nighthawk Trail.

Assuming you choose to continue the loop, follow the Nelson Loop Trail through the usual open meadows, but be more careful to watch your footing from this point onward, since the trail has an alarming tendency to dip near its center, due to erosion. Also, there are significantly more exposed rocks. Turn left onto the Bitterbrush Trail at mile 5.9 (6430) and follow it downhill to a junction with the Antelope Trail at mile 7.3 (6080), where you stay right to remain on the Bitterbrush Trail. Follow it the remaining distance to the parking lot, which you will find at mile 9.5 (5470).

4   Heil Ranch

*O*ne of the finest trail runs near Boulder; due to the fact that it has been open to the public for fewer years than other trails, its running surface is in superb shape and is less eroded. Its distance from Boulder also makes it the perfect place for a quiet run as fewer runners are attracted to it.

Winding up from the trailhead on the Wapiti Trail.
(Gretchen Hanisch)

Rating

Moderate

Location: 10.0 miles north of Boulder.
Distance/Type: 7.7 miles out and back
Running Time: 1.5 hours
Starting Elevation: 5,900 feet
Elevation Gain: 990 feet
Best Season: Spring into Winter
Jurisdiction: Boulder County Parks & Open Space (Heil Valley Ranch)
Maps: *Trails Illustrated # 100*
Permits/Fees: None

Mileage

0.0 Start north out of the parking lot onto the Wapiti Trail.
0.5 Stay north on Wapiti Trail avoiding Lichen Loop.
2.6 Bear northeast onto Ponderosa Loop.
5.1 Rejoin Wapiti Trail heading south.
7.7 Arrive at the trailhead.

Grade: An average angle of ascent of five degrees with no especially steep sections. Though most people should be able to run the entire course without stopping, be sure to watch out for loose rocks, of which there are many.

Getting There: From the intersection of 28th Street and Canyon Boulevard in Boulder, drive north on Route 36 for 8.3 miles and then turn left onto Lefthand Canyon Road. Drive west on Lefthand Canyon Road for 0.7 miles. Turn right (north) onto Geer Canyon Drive and follow it for 1.2 miles to the parking lot, which is on the right.

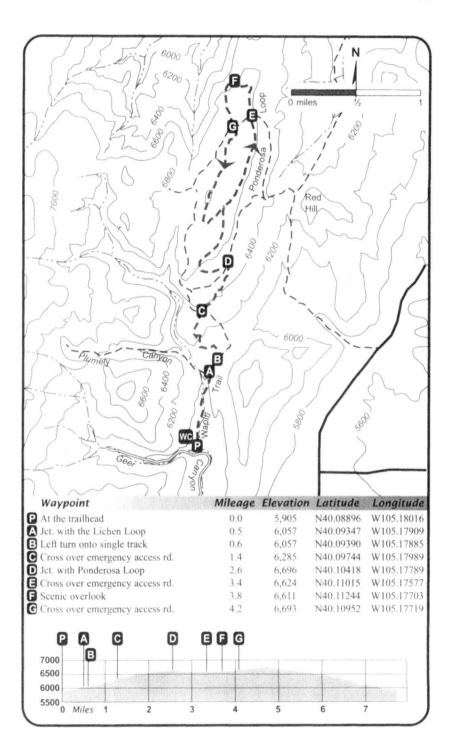

Waypoint	Mileage	Elevation	Latitude	Longitude
P At the trailhead	0.0	5,905	N40.08896	W105.18016
A Jct. with the Lichen Loop	0.5	6,057	N40.09347	W105.17909
B Left turn onto single track	0.6	6,057	N40.09390	W105.17885
C Cross over emergency access rd.	1.4	6,285	N40.09744	W105.17989
D Jct. with Ponderosa Loop	2.6	6,696	N40.10418	W105.17789
E Cross over emergency access rd.	3.4	6,624	N40.11015	W105.17577
F Scenic overlook	3.8	6,611	N40.11244	W105.17703
G Cross over emergency access rd.	4.2	6,693	N40.10952	W105.17719

The Route Description

Take the Wapiti Trail leading out of the north end of the parking lot. It switches from single track to a dirt road almost immediately, which heads north past a junction with the Lichen Loop at mile 0.5 (6060). Stay on the dirt road until mile 0.6, where the Wapiti Trail branches off to the left, switching back to single track. The trail crosses a small bridge in a meadow and then enters a forest, where it stays for most of the run. The trail becomes somewhat rocky in this area, following a steady uphill course until mile 2.6 (6700), where it reaches the Ponderosa Loop. This loop can be run in either direction. The remaining directions assume that you stay right at this junction and follow a counter-clockwise route.

The trail slabs across the side of a gentle hill, crossing an emergency access road at mile 3.4 (6620) and then curling around to the west and south until it reaches a fine viewpoint with benches at mile 3.8 (6610). Stop for a moment to admire the view to the west, and then continue along the backside of the loop, crossing the emergency access road at mile 4.2 (6690). Finish the loop and follow the Wapiti Trail back to the trailhead, which is at mile 7.7 (5900).

Admire the views at Heil Ranch

Rabbit Mountain   5

Wildflowers in bloom at the junction with Eagle Wind Loop.

The trail provides another excellent introduction to the sport. Although the trail can be rocky, it still is a pleasant area for a run. The views along the front range are absolutely superb, so be sure to take a rest and enjoy a few of them.

Rating

Easy

Location: 18.0 miles north of Boulder.
Distance/Type: 3.8 miles out and back
Running Time: 45 minutes
Starting Elevation: 5,480 feet
Elevation Gain: 410 feet
Best Season: Nearly year-round
Jurisdiction: Boulder County Parks & Open Space (Rabbit Mountain)
Map(s): Trails Illustrated # 100
Permits/Fees: None

Grade: An easy four degree angle of ascent. However, the footing can be rocky. A fall onto the sharp rocks that litter numerous sections of this trail could cause serious injuries.

Getting There: From the intersection of 28th Street and Canyon Boulevard in Boulder, drive north on Route 36 for 14.2 miles to the intersection with Route 66. Turn right onto Route 66 and drive 1.0 miles east to 53rd Street. Turn right onto 53rd Street, follow it for 2.8 miles, and turn right into the parking area.

GO

Mileage
0.0 Start north out of the parking lot.
0.5 Turn east onto the Eagle Wind Trail.
1.0 Bear east (left) on the Eagle Wind Trail Loop.
2.8 Rejoin three-way intersection and end of loop.
3.8 Arrive at parking lot.

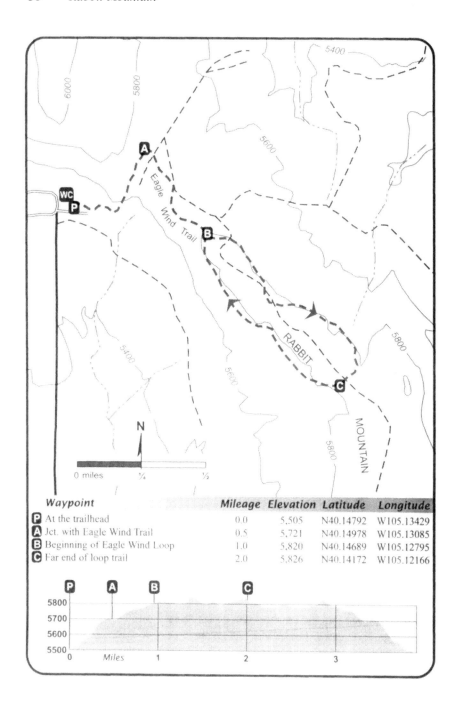

Waypoint	Mileage	Elevation	Latitude	Longitude
P At the trailhead	0.0	5,505	N40.14792	W105.13429
A Jct. with Eagle Wind Trail	0.5	5,721	N40.14978	W105.13085
B Beginning of Eagle Wind Loop	1.0	5,820	N40.14689	W105.12795
C Far end of loop trail	2.0	5,826	N40.14172	W105.12166

High peaks of the Front range are in view along the trail.

The Route Description

Take the trail leading out of the north side of the parking lot, which quickly traverses up an open hillside over loose rocks. Turn right at mile 0.5 (5720) onto the Eagle Wind Trail. The trail crosses a dirt road after about 100 yards and then continues east across an open meadow. Follow the trail uphill until a three-way junction at mile 1.0 (5820), where the Eagle Wind Trail goes both left and right; this is the start of a short loop trail. It can be run in either direction, though these directions assume a left turn for a clockwise loop. Follow the trail uphill through scrub pine trees and small meadows. It reaches its furthest eastern extent at mile 2.0 (5830), where there is a fine meadow overlook. Continue around the trail to the three-way junction previously described for the Eagle Wind Trail. From there, follow the trail back to the parking lot, which is at mile 3.8 (5510).

6 Anne U. White Trail

*T*his breathtakingly beautiful run is situated along
*Four Mile Creek. Although
there are no views of the
surrounding area,
the towering
canyon walls pro-
vide not only a
cool and refresh-
ing place to run,
but a home to an
abundant variety
of Colorado wild-
flowers to enjoy as
you make you way
along the trail.*

*Four Mile Creek at the
Trailhead. (Gretchen Hanisch)*

Rating

Easy

Location: 5.0 miles northwest of Boulder
Distance/Type: 3.3 miles out and back
Running Time: 45 minutes
Starting Elevation: 6,015 feet
Elevation Gain: 420 feet
Best Season: Nearly year-round
Jurisdiction: Boulder County Parks & Open Space
(Four Mile Canyon Creek)
Map(s): *Trails Illustrated # 100*
Permits/Fees: None

Mileage *GO*

0.0 Start west from
the trailhead.
1.65 Turn around and
head east.
3.3 Arrive at the trailhead.

Grade: An average five degree angle of ascent over
generally well-maintained trail. There is some sandy
trail surface, as well as occasional embedded rocks.

Getting There: From the corner of 28th Street and
Canyon Boulevard in Boulder, drive north on 28th
Street for 4.0 miles until Route 7 merges in on the
left. Turn south onto Route 7 (Broadway) and then
turn right onto Lee Hill Road after 0.2 miles. Follow
Lee Hill Road for 1.0 miles and then turn left onto
Wagonwheel Gap Road. The street sign is on the east

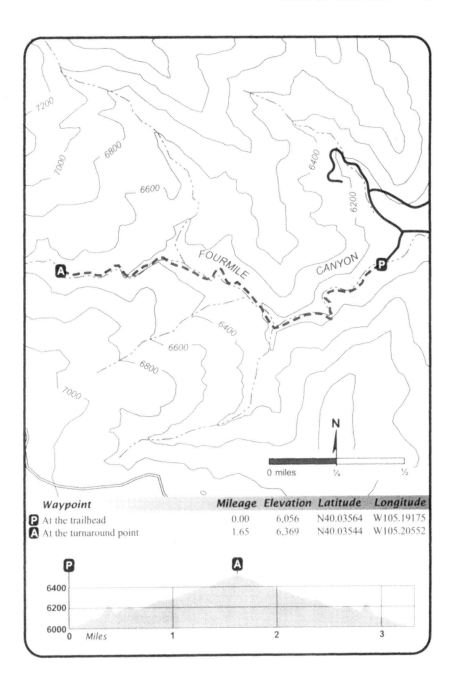

Waypoint	Mileage	Elevation	Latitude	Longitude
P At the trailhead	0.00	6,056	N40.03564	W105.19175
A At the turnaround point	1.65	6,369	N40.03544	W105.20552

side of the junction, and is difficult to see. If you see Lee Hill Road turn sharply left and uphill at a three-way intersection, you have gone too far. Once on Wagonwheel Gap Road, follow it for 1.0 miles and then turn left onto Pinto Drive and follow it for 0.2 miles to reach the parking area.

The Route Description

From the trailhead, follow the generally well-maintained trail alongside a stream bed as it travels west through Four Mile Canyon. The trail crosses the stream bed several times, which is only a problem during periods of very high water. There are no side trails, so just follow the Anne U. White trail until you reach a prominent "End of Trail" marker at mile 1.65 (6370). Then turn around and run back to the parking lot, which you will reach at mile 3.3 (6060).

Betasso Preserve Loop 7

Running along the Betasso Preserve Loop..

*A*n exceptional trail that winds through ponderosa pine forest, meadows, streams and provides many scenic views of the canyons below. Very popular with bikers, so run this trail on Saturdays and Wednesdays when they are not allowed in the preserve.

Rating

Easy

Location: 6.0 miles west of Boulder.
Distance/Type: 3.4 miles loop
Running Time: 45 minutes
Starting Elevation: 6,530 feet
Elevation Gain: 480 feet
Best Season: March through November
Jurisdiction: Boulder County Parks & Open Space
(Betasso Preserve)
Map(s): Trails Illustrated # 100
Permits/Fees: None

Grade: A scattering of rocky sections, and some sand near the parking area. Assuming a clockwise loop, the trail drops throughout the first half of the run, is flat for a short time, and regains the elevation loss during the final mile.

Getting There: Travel 5.1 miles west on Route 119 from 28th Street in Boulder and turn right onto Sugarloaf Road. Follow this road for 0.9 miles and then turn right onto Betasso Road. Follow Betasso for 0.5 mile and turn left into the Betasso Preserve access road. Follow the road to the parking lot.

Mileage

0.0 Turn west onto Canyon Loop Trail.
2.8 Continue south on Canyon Loop Trail.
3.4 Arrive at the parking lot.

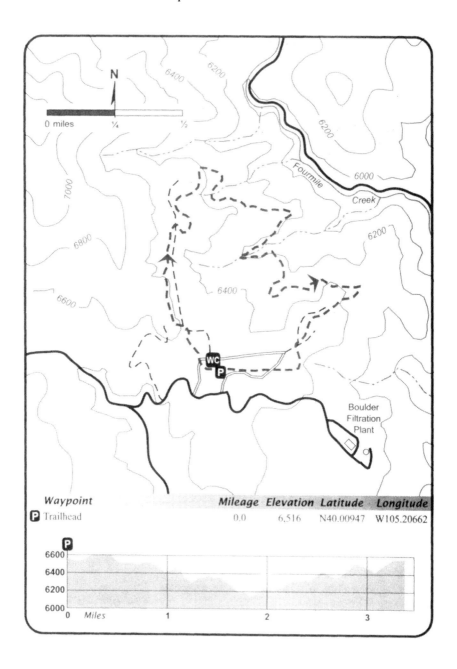

Waypoint	Mileage	Elevation	Latitude	Longitude
P Trailhead	0.0	6,516	N40.00947	W105.20662

Running through open stands of pine at Betasso Preserve.

The Route Description

This route assumes a clockwise circuit of the Betasso Preserve. From the trailhead, take the trail to the left and follow it up a short hill through an open field, where it enters a stand of pine trees and then becomes rocky as it drops 100 feet over the next few tenths of a mile and then jumps back up sixty vertical feet to a small ridge. From here, the trail drops without interruption until mile 1.8 (6170), where it reaches its lowest point. The trail then stays flat for a ¼ of a mile before embarking on a gradual and continuous ascent along a hillside covered with pine trees until it reaches a small spur trail at mile 2.8 (6490), where one can split off to the left for views of a nearby valley. The trail continues uphill until it reaches the parking area at mile 3.4 (6520).

8 Glacier Lake Road

*T*his route actually has the less glamourous name of Forest Road 120, so it is given the more scenic "Glacier Lake" name, based on the lake hidden to the north of its western terminus. Since this is not a trail, and is an actual road, be aware of the infrequent motorized traffic while running. It is still a very pleasant run, especially on the return trip, so enjoy.

A glimpse of the Indian Peaks from half way along Glacier Lake Road..

Rating

Moderate

Location: 12.0 miles west of Boulder.
Distance/Type: 10.8 miles out and back
Running Time: 2.0 hours
Starting Elevation: 8,441 feet
Elevation Gain: 640 feet
Best Season: May through October
Jurisdiction: Roosevelt National Forest
Map(s): *Trail Illustrated #102*
Permits/Fees: None

GO

Mileage

0.0 Start west out of the parking lot onto Forest Rd. 120. Head west and straight throughout the run.
5.4 Turn around at Route 72 intersection. Go East.
10.8 Arrive at parking lot.

Grade: An easy two degree uphill angle of ascent on the outbound leg of this road. There are few rocks and no roots to dodge. The slight angle of descent on the return leg makes for a very pleasant run.

Getting There: Travel 5.1 miles west on Route 119 from 28th Street in Boulder and turn right onto Sugarloaf Road. Go north on this road for 4.6 miles and turn right onto Sugarloaf Mountain Road. Follow this road for 0.8 miles to the obvious parking area.

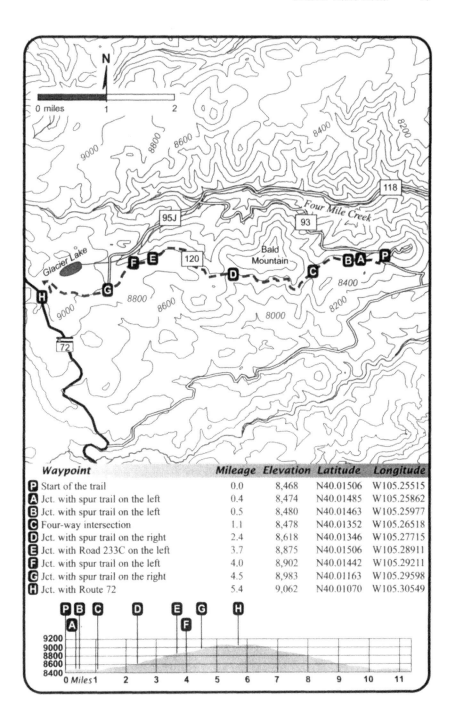

Waypoint		Mileage	Elevation	Latitude	Longitude
P	Start of the trail	0.0	8,468	N40.01506	W105.25515
A	Jct. with spur trail on the left	0.4	8,474	N40.01485	W105.25862
B	Jct. with spur trail on the left	0.5	8,480	N40.01463	W105.25977
C	Four-way intersection	1.1	8,478	N40.01352	W105.26518
D	Jct. with spur trail on the right	2.4	8,618	N40.01346	W105.27715
E	Jct. with Road 233C on the left	3.7	8,875	N40.01506	W105.28911
F	Jct. with spur trail on the left	4.0	8,902	N40.01442	W105.29211
G	Jct. with spur trail on the right	4.5	8,983	N40.01163	W105.29598
H	Jct. with Route 72	5.4	9,062	N40.01070	W105.30549

Traffic is light to non-existent on this dirt road.

The Route Description

There are several roads leading out of the parking area, so be careful about your initial route selection. The correct road is the first road branching off from the parking lot on the left, which is actually before the parking area. Follow the wide dirt road due west to mile 0.4 (8470), where there is a spur trail going left. Continue straight. There is another spur trail going left at mile 0.5 (8480). Again, go straight ahead on the main road. Go straight through a four-way intersection at mile 1.1 (8480).

Go straight when a spur trail appears at mile 2.4 (8620). For the next mile, there are good views to the right of the Indian Peaks area. Road 233C will appear on the left at mile 3.7 (8880); go straight on the main road, as usual. From here to the turn-around point, there are many private properties and driveways on both sides of the road.

Ignore a spur trail branching off to the left at mile 4.0 (8900). A major road branches off to the right at mile 4.5 (8980); ignore this as well and continue straight to the road's intersection with Route 72 at mile 5.4 (9060). In case you hadn't noticed, the basic instruction for this run is to go straight ahead and ignore all spur trails. Turn around and run back down a pleasant, gradual downhill incline to your car at mile 10.8 (8470).

Hogback Loop 9

Runner coming through the tunnel underneath Hwy 36 at Hogback Loop. (Gretchen Hanisch)

This is a short, hard workout worthy of multiple laps. It is best done in the morning and in non-inclement weather as it is in a wide open area. There are some great peak views towards the northern end of the loop for you to enjoy.

Rating

Easy

Location: Just outside the Boulder city limits on its northern fringe.

Distance/Type: 2.8 miles loop

Running Time: 45 minutes

Starting Elevation: 5,545 feet

Elevation Gain: 850 feet

Best Season: Nearly year-round

Jurisdiction: City of Boulder Open Space & Mtn. Parks

Map(s): *Trails Illustrated # 100*

Permits/Fees: None

Grade: This is rated as a beginner trail because of the short distance, but beware of the steep ascent midway through the run, which nearly gives this route an intermediate ranking. The ascent can be as steep as a 15% angle. There are few loose rocks, but many embedded ones.

Getting There: From the corner of 28th Street and Canyon Boulevard in Boulder, drive north on 28th Street for 4.0 miles until Route 7 merges in on the left. Then take the next dirt road on the right, a matter of an extra hundred yards, and drive 0.2 miles to the Foothills Trailhead parking area on the left side of the road.

GO

Mileage

0.0 Take Foothills Trail west out of the parking lot.

0.6 Turn north onto the Hogback Loop Trail.

2.2 Rejoin the Foothills Trail and head east.

2.8 Arrive at the parking lot.

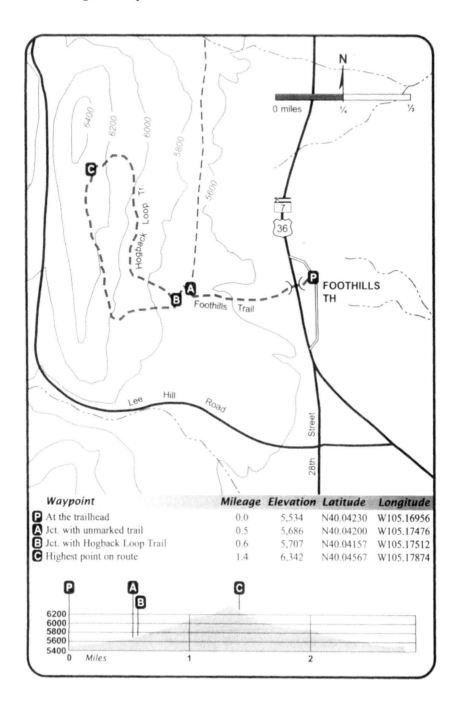

Waypoint	Mileage	Elevation	Latitude	Longitude
P At the trailhead	0.0	5,534	N40.04230	W105.16956
A Jct. with unmarked trail	0.5	5,686	N40.04200	W105.17476
B Jct. with Hogback Loop Trail	0.6	5,707	N40.04157	W105.17512
C Highest point on route	1.4	6,342	N40.04567	W105.17874

The Route Description

Take the Foothills Trail west out of the parking lot and run through the tunnel underneath Route 36. Continue until mile 0.5 (5690), where you stay left as an unmarked trail splits away to the north (see the Foothills Extension Trail description). Continue up a steep incline to mile 0.6 (5710), where you turn right onto the Hogback Loop Trail. After fifty yards, the trail splits. Take either the left or right turn in order to complete the loop. If you turn left, the ascent is over somewhat more wooden and stone steps, while a right turn leads you along more switch backing trail and fewer steps - pick your poison. Either way, the ascent is relatively steep. The high point of the run is at the far northern end of the loop at mile 1.4 (6340). Complete the loop and retrace your steps back to the parking lot, located at mile 2.8 (5530).

10 Meyers Homestead Trail

*A*n, easy and convenient workout located not too far from Boulder. You can use this as a quick run or a warm-up and continue down the road to address the more robust Walker Ranch Loop (Run # 14).

Just past the big red barn on Meyer Homestead Trail.

Rating

Easy

Classics

Location: 8.0 miles west of Boulder
Distance/Type: 5.2 miles out and back
Running Time: 1.0 hour
Starting Elevation: 7,730 feet
Elevation Gain: 840 feet
Best Season: March through November
Jurisdiction: Boulder County Parks & Open Space (Walker Ranch Park)
Map(s): *Trails Illustrated # 100*
Permits/Fees: None

Mileage

0.0 Head northwest on the Meyer Homestead Trail.
2.6 Trail ends so turn around and head southeast.
5.2 Arrive at the parking lot.

Grade: Moderate, with a 6 degree average angle of ascent. The trail is moderately well-maintained double track, with few rocks. The trail becomes somewhat sandy over its final quarter mile near the turn-around point.

Getting There: From the intersection of Route 36 and Baseline Road in Boulder, go west for 8.0 miles on Baseline Road, which becomes Flagstaff Road as it ascends over Flagstaff Mountain. Turn right into the parking lot just after the park sign.

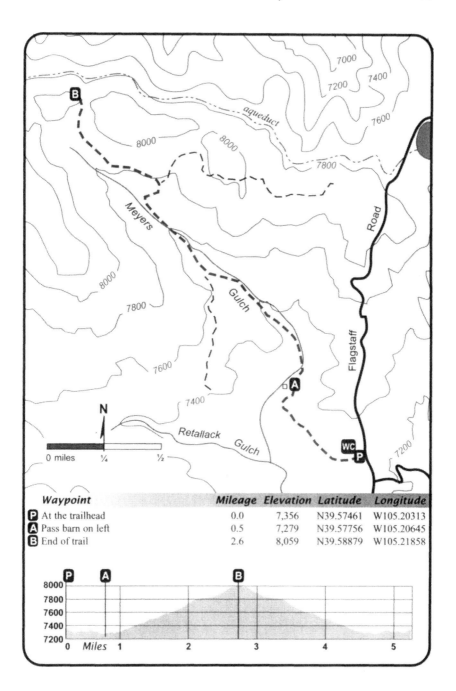

Waypoint	Mileage	Elevation	Latitude	Longitude
P At the trailhead	0.0	7,356	N39.57461	W105.20313
A Pass barn on left	0.5	7,279	N39.57756	W105.20645
B End of trail	2.6	8,059	N39.58879	W105.21858

The trail is a well-maintained double track.

The Route Description

From the trailhead, go northwest on the Meyers Homestead Trail. This is a double track trail with firm footing. The trail descends slightly, with good views on the left, until you pass a decidedly antique-looking barn on the left at mile 0.5 (7280). The trail continues at a steady uphill angle for another two miles, wending through meadows and open pine forests. The trail ends at mile 2.6 (8060), where you can stop at an overlook before turning around for a brisk and easy run back to the trailhead, which you will reach at mile 5.2 (7360).

Mount Sanitas/Dakota Ridge 11

View along Mount Sanitas Ridge with Green Mountain in the background.

This is a fiendish trail, despite the number of people who actually run laps on it. It is not only a great workout, but the views it offers of the Indian Peaks Wilderness to the west and the city of Boulder to the east are spectacular.

Location: Overlooks downtown Boulder.
Distance/Type: 3.2 miles loop
Running Time: 1.0 hour
Starting Elevation: 5,700 feet
Elevation Gain: 1,240 feet
Best Season: Nearly year-round
Map(s): *Trails Illustrated #100*
Jurisdiction: City of Boulder Open Space & Mtn. Parks (Boulder Mountain Park)
Permits/Fees: None

Grade: This is the shortest trail with a "difficult" rating in the entire book, and with good reason. The run up Mount Sanitas is at an average 18 degree angle of ascent, which includes rough rocks, ledges, roots, and any other obstacle you can think of. The final mile back to the trailhead along the Dakota Ridge trail is easy beginner material, but the trick is getting there.

Getting There: From the intersection of 28th Street and Canyon Boulevard, take Canyon westbound for 1.1 miles and then turn right (north) onto Broadway. Follow Broadway for 0.4 miles and then turn left onto Mapleton Avenue. Follow Mapleton west for 0.7 miles, and park on the right side of the street just past the Boulder Community Hospital.

Rating

Difficult

GO

Mileage

0.0 Begin at the Sanitas Valley trailhead.
0.1 Turn west onto Mt. Sanitas Trail.
1.1 Bear east on Mt. Sanitas East Ridge Trail.
1.4 Avoid trail heading north.
1.6 Turn south on Dakota Ridge Trail.
2.7 Connect with Valley Trail.
3.2 Arrive at parking lot.

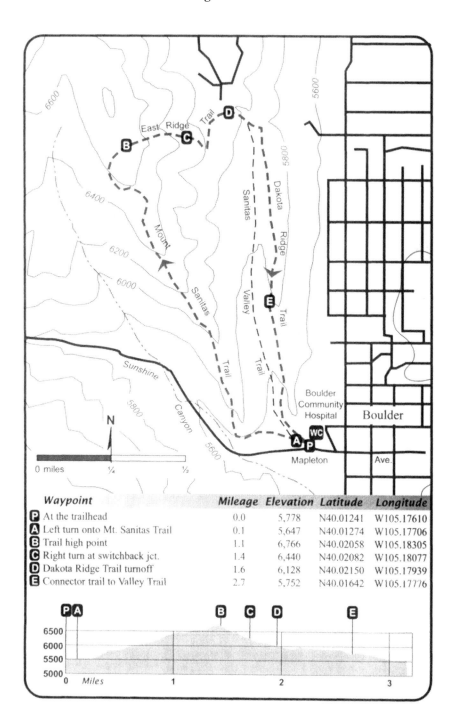

Waypoint	Mileage	Elevation	Latitude	Longitude
P At the trailhead	0.0	5,778	N40.01241	W105.17610
A Left turn onto Mt. Sanitas Trail	0.1	5,647	N40.01274	W105.17706
B Trail high point	1.1	6,766	N40.02058	W105.18305
C Right turn at switchback jct.	1.4	6,440	N40.02082	W105.18077
D Dakota Ridge Trail turnoff	1.6	6,128	N40.02150	W105.17939
E Connector trail to Valley Trail	2.7	5,752	N40.01642	W105.17776

Dogs are allowed off-leash on the trails around Mount Sanitas

The Route Description

Take the Sanitas Valley Trail from the trailhead. At mile 0.1 (5650), turn left onto the Mount Sanitas Trail and commence a brutal ascent. Expect every obstacle imaginable. This is a very rough trail, and deserves to be walked in many places. Reach the trail high point at mile 1.1 (6770), where the trail promptly plunges back down the east face of the peak along the Mount Sanitas East Ridge Trail. Do not take the vague trail that wanders away north from the high point.

The descent is no better than the ascent. Be extremely careful on the rocky ledges. There are also more loose rocks on this side of the peak. At mile 1.4 (6440), turn right where a side trail comes in on the left. This will keep you on the main trail. At mile 1.6 (6130), you will reach the bottom of the peak, where you are free to swear off running and take up knitting instead. If you have any resolve left, follow the trail as it curls around to the right (south), becoming a broad and manicured path. A wise choice is a left turn onto the Dakota Ridge Trail, which offers a pleasant run through a pine forest paralleling the Valley Trail. Ignore two connector trails back to the Valley Trail, taking instead the third one at mile 2.7 (5750), which is distinguished by a fence on the right side of the trail. The short connector brings you back to the Valley Trail, from which it is a short run south back to the parking lot, located at mile 3.2 (5780).

12 Sourdough Trail

An extremely popular trail, which has caused some ero-sion to occur. However, this trail is the perfect choice for a hot day due to its higher elevation and the fact that it is shaded by pine trees for the entire length of the run. Take pleasure in the cool temperatures and easy angle of ascent.

The Sourdough Trail is still snow covered through the spring. (Gretchen Hanisch)

Rating

Difficult

Location: 24.0 miles west of Boulder, off Route 72.
Distance/Type: 12.0 miles out and back
Running Time: 2.5 hours
Starting Elevation: 9,210 feet
Elevation Gain: 1,380 feet
Best Season: June through September
Jurisdiction: Roosevelt National Forest
Maps: *Trails Illustrated # 102*
Permits/Fees: None

Mileage

0.0 Begin north on Sourdough Trail.
1.8 Continue north on Sourdough Trail.
6.0 Turn around, south, at Brainard Lake Road.
12.0 Arrive back at parking lot.

Grade: The angle of ascent is only four degrees on this out-and-back trail, but it appears much harder due to the rocky tread, which can be severe in places. Be sure to use your most stable running shoes for this trail, since there is a strong chance of turning an ankle.

Getting There: From the intersection of Canyon and 28th Street in Boulder, travel west on Canyon (Route 119) for 16.6 miles to the rotary in Nederland. Take the Route 72 turnoff from that rotary, which heads west and then north out of Nederland. Follow Route 72 for 6.8 miles and take a left turn following

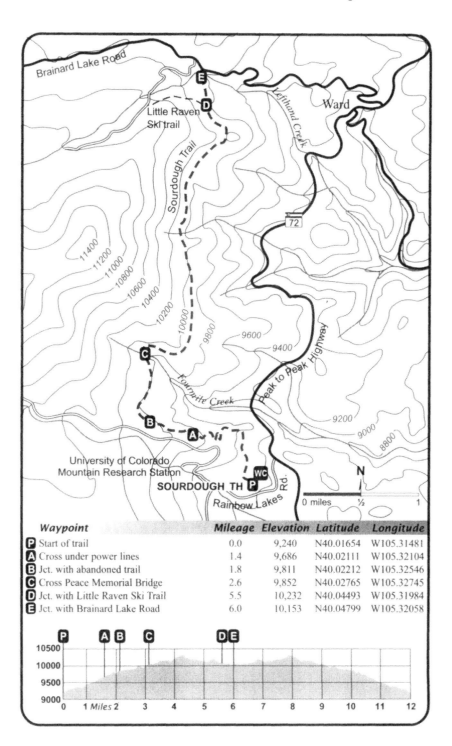

Waypoint		Mileage	Elevation	Latitude	Longitude
P	Start of trail	0.0	9,240	N40.01654	W105.31481
A	Cross under power lines	1.4	9,686	N40.02111	W105.32104
B	Jct. with abandoned trail	1.8	9,811	N40.02212	W105.32546
C	Cross Peace Memorial Bridge	2.6	9,852	N40.02765	W105.32745
D	Jct. with Little Raven Ski Trail	5.5	10,232	N40.04493	W105.31984
E	Jct. with Brainard Lake Road	6.0	10,153	N40.04799	W105.32058

the sign for the University of Colorado Mountain Research Station. Go west down this road for 0.5 miles and turn left into the large parking lot.

The Route Description

From the parking lot, cross the road to the north, where the trailhead is located. Run north along the rough trail and then through a series of switchbacks as the trail gains a modest amount of elevation. It passes under power lines at mile 1.4 (9690). An abandoned trail merges in on the left at mile 1.8 (9810). Continue through sporadically rough trail sections to the Peace Memorial Bridge at mile 2.6 (9850). For the next few miles, the trail becomes smoother as it skirts along the east side of Niwot Mountain. There is a junction with the Little Raven Ski Trail at mile 5.5 (10230); continue straight ahead on the Sourdough Trail. The trail maintenance improves considerably near its northern junction with the Brainard Lake Road. Stop at mile 6.0 (10150) where the trail crosses the road, and head back for six miles to your car, located at mile 12.0 (9240). The trail can also be run in reverse from the Brainard Lake Road, but this requires an uphill run on the return leg.

Teller Farms Trails 13

Crossing Boulder Creek Bridge.

*D*ue to the lack of tree cover on this route, it is not ideal for a hot day. Also, the wet areas near several fields and ponds along the route are mosquito breeding grounds, so be careful. However, this run offers excellent views of the mountains and plains of Boulder.

Rating

Moderate

Location: 5.0 miles east of Boulder
Distance/Type: 12.0 miles out and back
Running Time: 2.5 hours, though speedsters can do it much faster.
Starting Elevation: 5,220 feet
Elevation Gain: 590 feet
Best Season: Nearly year-round
Jurisdiction: City of Boulder Open Space & Mtn. Parks
Map(s): *Trails Illustrated # 100*
Permits/Fees: None

Grade: An easy intermediate, with smooth trails and low angles of ascent. The only challenge for a beginner is the distance, but since this is an out-and-back trail, you can turn around at any time.

Getting There: Travel 5.1 miles east on Arapahoe Road from 28th Street, then turn left at the Teller Farm sign and drive 0.5 miles north to the parking lot.

Mileage

0.0 Start northeast out of the parking lot.
0.2 Bear east on Teller Farms Trail.
2.1 Continue northeast out of parking lot and cross road.
4.8 Continue north and then go west on trail.
6.0 Turnaround at trail end heading east and south.
12.0 Arrive back at parking lot.

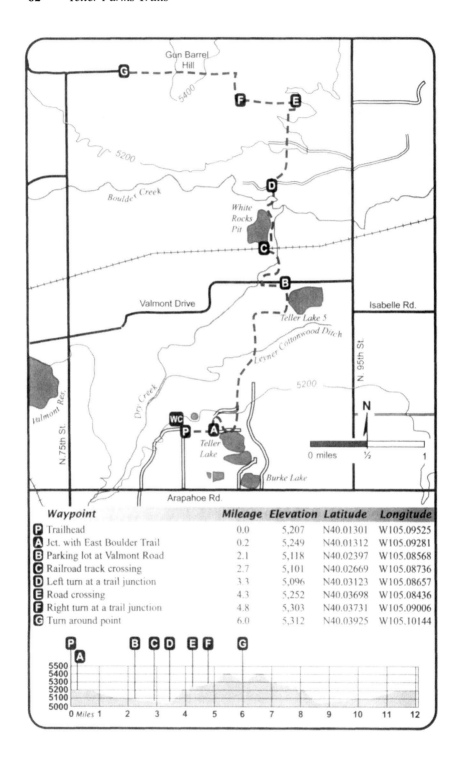

Waypoint	Mileage	Elevation	Latitude	Longitude
P Trailhead	0.0	5,207	N40.01301	W105.09525
A Jct. with East Boulder Trail	0.2	5,249	N40.01312	W105.09281
B Parking lot at Valmont Road	2.1	5,118	N40.02397	W105.08568
C Railroad track crossing	2.7	5,101	N40.02669	W105.08736
D Left turn at a trail junction	3.3	5,096	N40.03123	W105.08657
E Road crossing	4.3	5,252	N40.03698	W105.08436
F Right turn at a trail junction	4.8	5,303	N40.03731	W105.09006
G Turn around point	6.0	5,312	N40.03925	W105.10144

The Route Description

Take the trail heading northeast from the parking lot. At a junction with the East Boulder Trail at mile 0.2 (5,250), stay to the right and follow the trail due east until it curls left at Teller Lake and heads north through farmer's fields. The trail ends at a parking lot on the south side of Valmont Road at mile 2.1 (5120). Continue through the parking lot and find a small trail leading out of its northwest corner. Run down this trail as it parallels the south side of Valmont Road until it reaches an obvious road crossing. Cross over Valmont at this point and continue north on the much wider trail through more fields. Cross over an abandoned railroad track at mile 2.7 (5100) and almost immediately pass the pleasant White Rocks Pit, which is actually a fine pond where deer are ducks are frequent visitors. Cross an excellent bridge over Boulder Creek just after the pond and continue to a trail junction at mile 3.3 (5100). Turn left here, cross over a small bridge after a few yards, and take an immediate right turn after the bridge to access a small single track trail that ascends a small hill. The trail turns due east about 2/3 of the way up the hill and skirts around to the east and then north, crossing a paved road at mile 4.3 (5250). Cross the road and continue through barren fields until you reach an unmarked trail junction at mile 4.8 (5300). A water tank will be located straight ahead. Turn right at this junction and follow the trail around to the north and then west as the trail ascends a low hill and passes to the right of the water tank. From here, it is an easy half-mile downhill jog to the trail end at a road crossing at mile 6.0 (5310). Turn around and head back to the parking lot for a complete circuit of 12.0 miles.

Several ponds dot the landscape at Teller Farms.

14 Walker Ranch Loop

*T*his route offers excellent views, particularly along the ridgeline near the end of the run. The trail also parallels beautiful South Boulder Creek for a short stretch beginning at about mile 1.0. It is an extremely popular trail, especially with mountain bikers, so just be heads up. As a trailrunner on this route, you are in the minority.

Running into the Ethel Harrold Trailhead.

Rating

Difficult

Mileage

0.0 Start southwest on South Boulder Trail.
1.4 Bear east onto Walker Ranch Loop.
2.5 Continue east on Crescent Meadow Trail.
5.8 Bear west to avoid Ethel Harrold connector.
7.5 Arrive at parking lot.

Location: 9.0 miles west of Boulder.
Distance/Type: 7.5 miles loop
Running Time: 1.5 hours
Starting Elevation: 7,235 feet
Elevation Gain: 1,730 feet
Best Season: March through November
Jurisdiction: Boulder County Parks & Open Space (Walker Ranch)
Maps(s): *Trails Illustrated # 100*
Permits/Fees: None

Grade: Do not let the short mileage fool you - this is a hard trail, and is well worth its "difficult" rating. There are two long uphill ascents, as well as lots of rocks, cliffs, and even deep sandy patches that will make you think you are running on a beach. Be careful and pay attention to your footing at all times.

Getting There: From the intersection of Route 36 and Baseline Road in Boulder, go west for 8.5 miles on Baseline Road, which becomes Flagstaff Road as

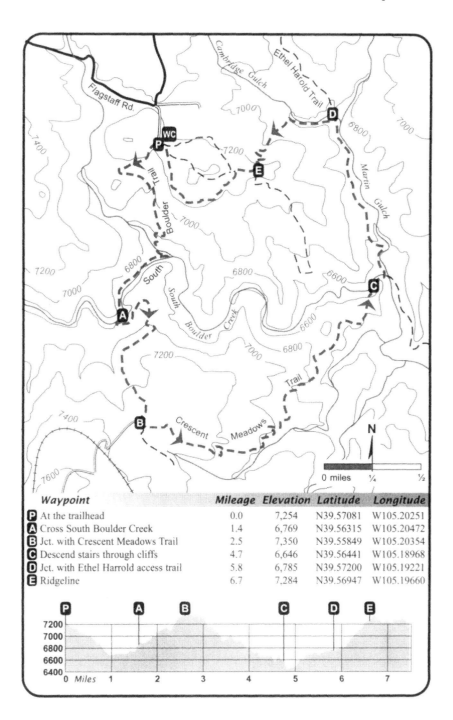

Waypoint		Mileage	Elevation	Latitude	Longitude
P	At the trailhead	0.0	7,254	N39.57081	W105.20251
A	Cross South Boulder Creek	1.4	6,769	N39.56315	W105.20472
B	Jct. with Crescent Meadows Trail	2.5	7,350	N39.55849	W105.20354
C	Descend stairs through cliffs	4.7	6,646	N39.56441	W105.18968
D	Jct. with Ethel Harrold access trail	5.8	6,785	N39.57200	W105.19221
E	Ridgeline	6.7	7,284	N39.56947	W105.19660

it ascends over Flagstaff Mountain. Turn left into the parking lot. Please note that there are two parking lots - follow the dirt road up and around a corner to reach the one closer to the trailhead.

The Route Description

From the trailhead, turn right onto the South Boulder Trail and commence a fast downhill run to the South Boulder Creek. Though the tread is generally good, there are rocky ledges and partially buried stones, so be careful of your footing. After a mile, the trail turns right and parallels South Boulder Creek on a wide, well graded trail. Catch your breath here, because the ascent is about to begin. Cross South Boulder Creek at mile 1.4 (6770), turn left at a fork just after the bridge, and begin to climb up the Walker Ranch Loop Trail. This ascent lasts for just over a mile, with three sharp uphill climbs broken by two short flat sections. The second flat stretch is especially well graded, and can mislead you into thinking the climb is over. It is not! You must reach the junction with the Crescent Meadow Trail at mile 2.5 (7350) to be through with the ascent.

The Crescent Meadows Trail takes you east through open meadows and then plunges into a pine forest where the trail becomes increasingly rocky. When you reach a "cliff warning" sign, stop running and carefully step down through a series of wooden steps at mile 4.7 (6650) until you reach South Boulder Creek. Then cross the creek a few hundred yards later and begin the ascent back to the parking lot. This is a slow section to run, featuring long uphill stretches of sand on double track trail, punctuated by clusters of embedded rocks. The torture comes to an end at mile 5.8 (6790), where you turn left to stay on the main trail and avoid the connector trail to the Ethel Harrold trailhead. Though the trail continues uphill from here, the amount of sand underfoot declines rapidly, while the trail becomes narrow single track and is hidden under pine trees, keeping the hot sun away. The trail breaks out onto a stunning, open ridge line at mile 6.7 (7280), with views both to the north and south. Continue along the ridge back to the parking lot, which you will reach at mile 7.5 (7250).

Community Ditch Trail 15

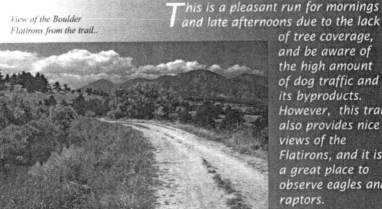

View of the Boulder
Flatirons from the trail.

This is a pleasant run for mornings and late afternoons due to the lack of tree coverage, and be aware of the high amount of dog traffic and its byproducts. However, this trail also provides nice views of the Flatirons, and it is a great place to observe eagles and raptors.

Rating

Easy

Location: 6.0 miles south of Boulder.
Distance/Type: 8.1 miles out and back
Running Time: 1.5 hours
Starting Elevation: 5,645 feet
Elevation Gain: 310 feet
Best Season: Nearly year-round
Jurisdiction: City of Boulder Open Space & Mtn. Parks
Map(s): Trails Illustrated # 100
Permits/Fees: None

Grade: Though the distance would normally justify an "intermediate" trail rating, the angle of ascent is so minimal that this deserves a "beginner" rating. Also, since this is an out-and-back route, you can turn around at any time to shorten the total mileage.

Getting There: From the intersection of 28th Street and Canyon Boulevard in Boulder, drive 1.1 miles west on Canyon Boulevard and then turn left (south) onto Broadway. Follow Broadway for 4.0 miles to the Eldorado Springs turnoff, which is Route 170. Turn right onto Route 170 and follow it west for 1.7 miles to the Doudy Draw Trailhead, which is on the left side of the road.

Mileage

0.0 Start south out of parking lot.
0.5 Head east onto Community Ditch Trail.
2.8 Bear east on the Community Ditch Trail.
3.6 Turn around or take Marshall Mesa Trail.
8.1 Arrive at parking lot.

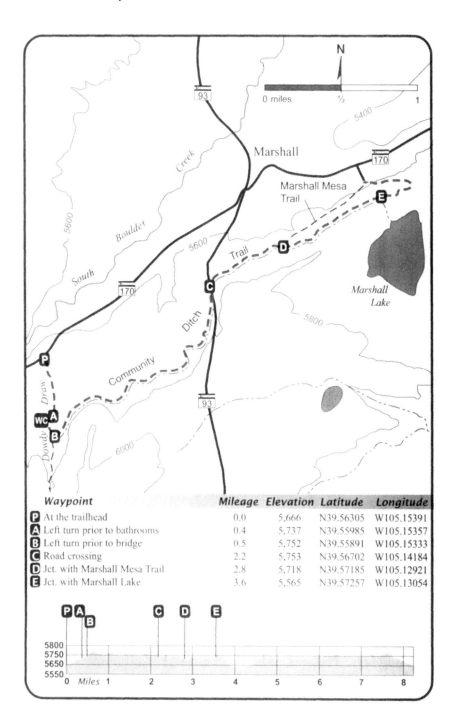

Waypoint	Mileage	Elevation	Latitude	Longitude
P At the trailhead	0.0	5,666	N39.56305	W105.15391
A Left turn prior to bathrooms	0.4	5,737	N39.55985	W105.15357
B Left turn prior to bridge	0.5	5,752	N39.55891	W105.15333
C Road crossing	2.2	5,753	N39.56702	W105.14184
D Jct. with Marshall Mesa Trail	2.8	5,718	N39.57185	W105.12921
E Jct. with Marshall Lake	3.6	5,565	N39.57257	W105.13054

The Route Description

From the parking lot, take the trail leading southbound. This is a paved path, but only until mile 0.4 (5740), where you take a left turn onto dirt single track just prior to bathroom facilities. A sign will note that this is the Community Ditch Trail as well as the Doudy Draw Trail. The Doudy Draw Trail soon departs, as it follows a bridge spanning a local irrigation ditch at mile 0.5 (5750). However, you will be turning left here to continue on the Community Ditch Trail, which stays to the north side of the ditch as the trail takes you east. There are great views of the Flatirons to your left and slightly behind you as you follow this route through open fields. The splendid views end at mile 2.2 (5750), where the solitude of the fields are replaced by the noise of a highway crossing. Be very careful when crossing to the far side of the road, since there is a great deal of traffic here.

Once safely across, continue on the trail, which appears a short distance to the north. Follow the trail east, always staying to the left (north) of the ditch, until mile 2.8 (5720), where the Marshall Mesa Trail drops away to the left. Ignore this junction and continue east on the Community Ditch Trail, which soon reaches the north side of Marshall Lake at mile 3.6 (5570). Run past the lake and follow the trail as it turns left and drops rapidly to the Marshall Mesa trailhead on Route 170. You can either retrace your steps back to the parking lot from this point, or take the Marshall Mesa Trail from the Marshall Mesa trailhead, which cuts off a few tenths of a mile on the return trip. If you take the long way back by retracing your steps, you will reach the parking area at mile 8.1 (5670).

Lack of tree coverage provides outstanding views but can be hot in summer.

16 Doudy Draw Trail

A pleasant and easy run with fine views of the Flatirons. Although the last mile leading east away from the mountains is a bit dull in the colder months, in the Spring the wildflowers are abundant.

Runner on the Doudy Draw Trail, south of the Community Ditch Trail.

Rating

Easy

Location: 6.0 miles south of Boulder.
Distance/Type: 6.2 miles out and back
Running Time: 1.25 hours
Starting Elevation: 5,665 feet
Elevation Gain: 690 feet
Best Season: Nearly year-round
Jurisdiction: City of Boulder Open Space & Mtn. Parks
Map(s): *Trails Illustrated # 100*
Permits/Fees: None

Grade: This trail has a 4% grade.

Mileage

0.0 Start south out of the parking lot.
0.5 Continue south on Doudy Draw Trail.
3.1 Turnaround at parking lot.
6.2 Arrive back at trailhead.

Getting There: From the intersection of 28th Street and Canyon Boulevard in Boulder, drive 1.1 miles west on Canyon Boulevard and then turn left (south) onto Broadway. Follow Broadway for 4.0 miles to the Eldorado Springs turnoff, which is Route 170. Turn right onto Route 170 and follow it west for 1.7 miles to the Doudy Draw Trailhead, which is on the left side of the road.

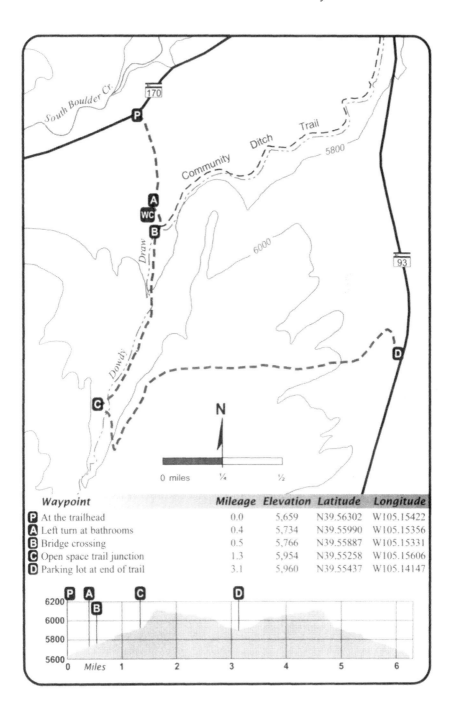

Waypoint	Mileage	Elevation	Latitude	Longitude
P At the trailhead	0.0	5,659	N39.56302	W105.15422
A Left turn at bathrooms	0.4	5,734	N39.55990	W105.15356
B Bridge crossing	0.5	5,766	N39.55887	W105.15331
C Open space trail junction	1.3	5,954	N39.55258	W105.15606
D Parking lot at end of trail	3.1	5,960	N39.55437	W105.14147

Except for one steep section, most of the Doudy Trail is a very gentle grade.

The Route Description

From the parking lot, take the trail leading southbound. This is a paved path, but only until mile 0.4 (5730), where you take a left turn onto dirt single track just prior to bathroom facilities. A sign will note that this is the Community Ditch Trail as well as the Doudy Draw Trail. Leave the Community Ditch Trail and cross at bridge at mile 0.5 (5770), where the trail heads south through open fields. The trail ascends slowly as it passes a junction with the Boulder County Open Space at mile 1.3 (5950), which can be ignored by following the trail to the left. Shortly thereafter, the trail enters a pleasant stand of pine trees as it switchbacks up a low ridge. Unfortunately, this leaves you with a boring slog to the east through open prairie and electrical towers to the parking lot at the far end of the trail at mile 3.1 (5960). To make matters worse, you must then negotiate a 200 vertical foot ascent up a hill immediately after turning around for the run back. However, don't worry - it is all downhill from there back to the trailhead at mile 6.2 (5660).

Enchanted Mesa Medley 17

View of the Flatirons from the Mesa Trail.

This run provides the occasional view of hot air balloons being launched at nearby Base Line Reservoir. Which is always a neat experience. However, the descent on Skunk Canyon Trail has some high steps. So if you have knees that can't take the impact, it's suggested you run this route in the opposite direction.

Rating

Easy

Location: 1.0 mile south of Boulder.
Distance/Type: 3.6 miles medley
Running Time: 45 minutes
Starting Elevation: 5,720 feet
Elevation Gain: 710 feet
Best Season: Nearly year-round
Jurisdiction: City of Boulder Open Space & Mtn. Parks (Boulder Mountain Park)
Map(s): *Trails Illustrated # 100*
Permits/Fees: None

Grade: A four degree average angle of ascent, but most of the ascents come in short bursts, so there is actually a fair amount of exercise required. The trail has some embedded rocks, through the return on the Enchanted Mesa Medley.

Getting There: From the intersection of Route 36 and Base Line Road at the south end of Boulder, drive west on Base Line Road for 1.0 miles, and turn left (south) onto 12th Street. Follow it for 0.2 miles, and turn right into a dirt parking area.

GO

Mileage

0.0 Start north and west on the McClintock Trail.
0.7 Head southwest on Mesa Trail.
0.9 Continue South on Mesa Trail.
1.5 Turn north on Skunk Canyon Trail.
2.3 Bear west on Kohler Mesa Trail.
2.5 Turn northeast on Enchanted Mesa Trail.
3.6 Arrive at parking lot.

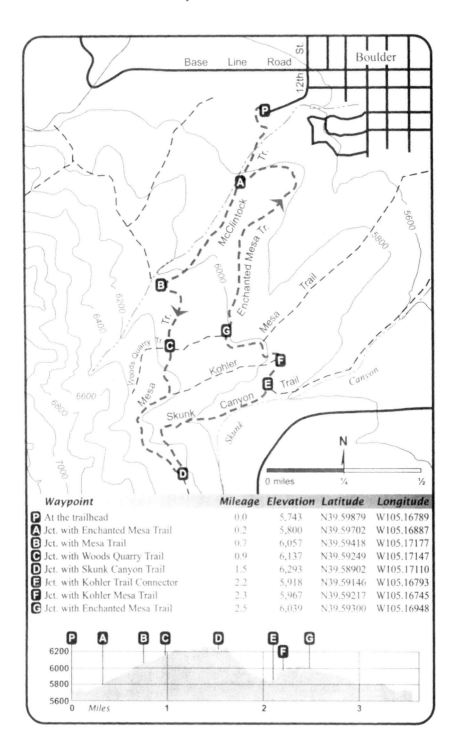

Waypoint		Mileage	Elevation	Latitude	Longitude
P	At the trailhead	0.0	5,743	N39.59879	W105.16789
A	Jct. with Enchanted Mesa Trail	0.2	5,800	N39.59702	W105.16887
B	Jct. with Mesa Trail	0.7	6,057	N39.59418	W105.17177
C	Jct. with Woods Quarry Trail	0.9	6,137	N39.59249	W105.17147
D	Jct. with Skunk Canyon Trail	1.5	6,293	N39.58902	W105.17110
E	Jct. with Kohler Trail Connector	2.2	5,918	N39.59146	W105.16793
F	Jct. with Kohler Mesa Trail	2.3	5,967	N39.59217	W105.16745
G	Jct. with Enchanted Mesa Trail	2.5	6,039	N39.59300	W105.16948

The Route Description

Take the McClintock Trail, which begins just up the hill from the parking area. After a hundred yards, turn right to remain on the trail at a "T" junction. This is a surprisingly jungle-like environment, with dense tree growth. Cross the Enchanted Mesa Trail at mile 0.2 (5560) to continue on the McClintock Trail, which picks up slightly to the right on the other side of the Enchanted Mesa Trail. Tree cover begins to thin out as the trail ascends rapidly. Turn left at mile 0.7 (5550) onto the Mesa Trail, and turn right at a junction located at mile 0.9 (5510) in order to remain on the Mesa Trail. Ignore a nearby right turn onto the Woods Quarry Trail. The trail begins to pass through small stretches of open meadow, yielding great views of the adjacent Flatirons. At mile 1.5 (5540), turn left onto the Skunk Canyon Trail, which drops over rather large wooden steps to a turnoff at mile 2.2 (5500) leading to the Kohler Mesa Trail. From this point, it is sometimes possible to see balloons being launched to the east from the region of Base Line Reservoir.

The access trail goes steeply uphill, at the crest of which you are confronted with a series of confusing trail junctions. The first junction is at mile 2.3 (5970) where you turn left at a Kohler Mesa Trail junction. Turn right at yet another Kohler Mesa Trail junction 100 yards later, and (surprise!) left at another Kohler Mesa Trail junction after another 100 yards. At this point, you are free of Kohler Mesa, and deserve to turn right onto the wide and exquisitely maintained Enchanted Mesa Trail at mile 2.5 (6040). From here, it is an easy jog downhill back to the parking area, which you will find at mile 3.6 (5740).

Parts of the trail are broad and well-maintained.

18 Mesa Trail Loop

This fine route just south of Boulder, popular with many local trail runners, is perhaps the best run in the Boulder area. Though there are a number of trail junctions, the route becomes obvious after a few repetitions.

The Mesa Trail is a favorite with the locals.

Rating

Moderate

Classics

Location: 6.0 miles south of Boulder, off CO-170
Distance/Type: 6.5 miles loop
Running Time: 1.25 hours
Starting Elevation: 5,620 feet
Elevation Gain: 880 feet
Best Season: Nearly year-round
Jurisdiction: Boulder Mountain Park
Map(s): *Trails Illustrated # 100*
Permits/Fees: None

Grade: A moderate climb from the trailhead and continuing for 2.5 miles. The trail is wide and smooth for the first two miles, gradually narrowing and including steps and embedded rocks. The downhill sections on the second half of the run are generally smoother.

Mileage *GO*

0.0 Start north on Mesa Trail.
2.8 Bear east on South Fork Trail.
3.5 Go east on North Fork Shanahan Trail.
4.3 Turn south on unmarked trail.
5.0 Join Big Bluestem Trail. Go South.
5.6 Rejoin Mesa Trail.
6.5 Arrive at trailhead.

Getting There: From the intersection of 28th Street and Canyon Boulevard in Boulder, drive 1.1 miles west on Canyon Boulevard and then turn left (south) onto Broadway. Follow Broadway for 4.0 miles to the Eldorado Springs turnoff, which is Route 170. Turn right onto Route 170 and follow it west for 1.7 miles to the Mesa Trailhead, which is on the right side of the road.

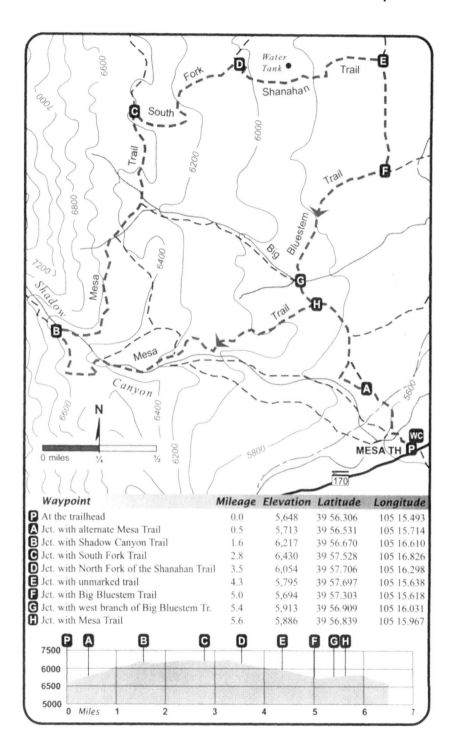

Waypoint	Mileage	Elevation	Latitude	Longitude
P At the trailhead	0.0	5,648	39 56.306	105 15.493
A Jct. with alternate Mesa Trail	0.5	5,713	39 56.531	105 15.714
B Jct. with Shadow Canyon Trail	1.6	6,217	39 56.670	105 16.610
C Jct. with South Fork Trail	2.8	6,430	39 57.528	105 16.826
D Jct. with North Fork of the Shanahan Trail	3.5	6,054	39 57.706	105 16.298
E Jct. with unmarked trail	4.3	5,795	39 57.697	105 15.638
F Jct. with Big Bluestem Trail	5.0	5,694	39 57.303	105 15.618
G Jct. with west branch of Big Bluestem Tr.	5.4	5,913	39 56.909	105 16.031
H Jct. with Mesa Trail	5.6	5,886	39 56.839	105 15.967

Boulder's magnificent Flatirons form the backdrop of the Mesa Trail.

The Route Description

Take the Mesa Trail north from the trailhead; you will cross a bridge immediately and then wind uphill. The trail is wide and well-maintained. Avoid a narrower version of the Mesa Trail at mile 0.5 (5710) by staying to the left. The trail continues to wind uphill until mile 1.6 (6220), where the Shadow Canyon Trail splits off to the left. Stay on the Mesa Trail as it narrows considerably and becomes much rougher, going up over rock stairs through pine forests. Turn sharply right at mile 2.8 (6430) onto the South Fork Trail, which widens at once and goes downhill almost due east. Turn right at mile 3.5 (6050) onto the north fork of the Shanahan Trail, which briefly veers south before heading east past a large green water tank (on the north side of the trail).

The tricky part of the route is to turn right onto an unmarked trail at mile 4.3 (5800). This trail branches off just before the Shanahan Trail turns sharply left (north). Though narrow, the trail is well-trodden. Follow it south through a gate and open fields until mile 5.0 (5690), where you turn right onto the Big Bluestem Trail. There will be another gate to negotiate a short ways down this trail. When a side branch of the trail bearing the same name splits away sharply to the right at mile 5.4 (5910) near a high voltage tower, stay on the main path, continuing south until mile 5.6 (5890), where you turn left to rejoin the Mesa Trail. The trailhead is all downhill from there, lying at mile 6.5 (5650).

Rattlesnake Gulch Trail 19

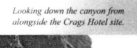
Looking down the canyon from alongside the Crags Hotel site.

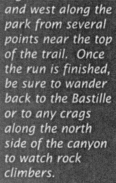

Despite the steepness of the ascent, there are great views east and west along the park from several points near the top of the trail. Once the run is finished, be sure to wander back to the Bastille or to any crags along the north side of the canyon to watch rock climbers.

Rating

Moderate

Location: 8.0 miles south of Boulder
Distance/Type: 4.7 miles loop
Running Time: 1.25 hours
Starting Elevation: 5,870 feet
Elevation Gain: 1,260 feet
Best Season: March through November
Jurisdiction: City of Boulder Open Space and Mtn. Parks (Eldorado State Canyon)
Map(s): *Trails Illustrated # 100*
Permits/Fees: $6 park pass

Grade: Intermediate, with a steep ascent from the beginning of the Rattlesnake Gulch Trail to the site of the former Crags Hotel. Of particular concern is the descent of the Rattlesnake Gulch loop trail located above the Crags Hotel site, which is full of loose rock.

Getting There: From the intersection of 28th Street and Canyon Boulevard in Boulder, drive 1.1 miles west on Canyon Boulevard and then turn left (south) onto Broadway. Follow Broadway for 4.0 miles to the Eldorado Springs turnoff, which is Route 170. Turn right onto Route 170 and follow it west for 3.2 miles to Eldorado State Park.

Mileage

0.0 Start west out of the parking lot.
0.5 Head slightly south and east on Fowler Trail.
0.7 Turn southwest on Rattlesnake Gulch Trail.
1.7 Head west at junction with loop.
3.0 Turn east at junction with the loop.
4.7 Arrive back at parking lot.

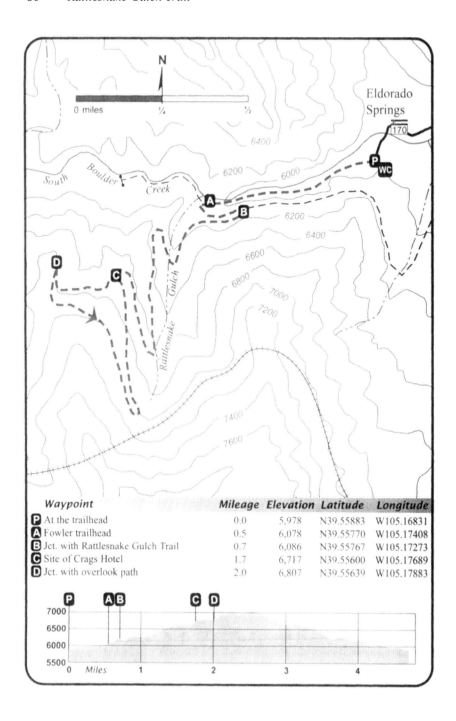

Waypoint	Mileage	Elevation	Latitude	Longitude
P At the trailhead	0.0	5,978	N39.55883	W105.16831
A Fowler trailhead	0.5	6,078	N39.55770	W105.17408
B Jct. with Rattlesnake Gulch Trail	0.7	6,086	N39.55767	W105.17273
C Site of Crags Hotel	1.7	6,717	N39.55600	W105.17689
D Jct. with overlook path	2.0	6,807	N39.55639	W105.17883

Looking up the canyon from along the Rattlesnake Gulch Trail.

The Route Description

Park immediately after passing through the park's ranger station. You could drive another 0.5 mile to the trailhead, but it is more fun to run up the main park road past the Bastille climbing area on your left, where you can literally touch rock climbers belaying their climbing partners higher up on this vertical wall. At mile 0.5 (6080), turn left into the trailhead area for the Fowler Trail. The trail begins on the left side of the parking area, and follows a wide, manicured path until mile 0.7 (6080), where you turn right onto the Rattlesnake Gulch Trail. Here, the trail is substantially less manicured, with rough footing and rocky ledges for the first few hundred yards. After that, there are fewer ledges but still plenty of rocks as the trail ascends rapidly through a series of switchbacks to the site of the former Crags Hotel at mile 1.7 (6720). Pause here for a breather and admire the view. Then continue straight ahead on the same trail to complete a counter-clockwise loop. There will be a trail leading to an observation overlook at mile 2.0 (6810). If you don't want the view, turn left instead to continue along the loop trail, which leads you gasping uphill with no breaks until it approaches a railroad track and then plunges down through loose rocks (slow down!) to return to the site of the Crags Hotel. Then turn right and retrace your path back to the trailhead, located at mile 4.7 (5980).

Denver Area

In alphabetical order, the trails
itemized in this section are as follows:

Denver Northwest

Apex Loop
Golden Gate Canyon Loop
White Ranch Loop

Denver West

Alderfer/Three Sisters Medley
Bergen Peak Loop
Buck Gulch Loop
Colorado/Green Mountain Trails
Elk Meadow Loop
Green Mountain Loop
Lair to Pence Connector Trail
Meyer Ranch Loop
Mount Falcon Loop
Mount Galbraith Loop
Red Rocks/Dakota Ridge Loop
Reynolds Park Loop
Shadow Mountain Loop
South Valley Park Medley

Denver Southwest

Carpenter Peak Trail
Plymouth Mountain Trail
Red Mesa Loop
Roxborough Park Medley

Denver South

Bluffs Park Loop
Castlewood Canyon Loop
High Line Canal Trail

*In Castlewood
Canyon State Park.*

In the Denver area, nearly all running trails are located in a narrow band of the foothills about ten miles deep, running north to south along the edge of the metropolitan region. An area of upthrust red rocks stretching over a ten-mile area to the southwest of C-470 is a particularly pleasant area for running. In addition, hot air balloons are a common sight in the early morning near Chatfield reservoir, which is also southwest of C-470. Runners on trails to the west of C-470 are likely to find at least some tree cover to protect them from the sun, but runners to the east of C-470 will have trouble even finding a tree - after all, Denver is technically located in a desert!

Runners to the northwest of Denver may notice an unusual smell in the air. It is hops, and blows from the Coors brewery located in Golden. When the wind is blowing from the east, runners on the Apex and Mount Galbraith trail circuits can experience quite an aroma.

Runners may occasionally find group events going on along their favorite trails. For example, the Colorado Mountain Club (CMC) may have as many as 17 trips going into the mountains on summer weekends, some of which will be in the foothills area. Also, Denver Trail Runners sponsors late afternoon runs, while Team Evergreen operates a variety of weekend mountain bike trips in the foothills. The CMC keeps its group sizes small, but the Team Evergreen outings can involve dozens of mountain bikers. It is worthwhile to check its web site at *www.teamevergreen.org* to see where the group will be, so you can run somewhere else.

The trail system near Denver suffers from some overuse, though it seems that Denver-area residents are stuck on only a few favorite trails. This section presents a number of trails on which I rarely see trail runners, even though these trails are better than many of the current favorites.

If you are looking for lots of trail running company, try the Elk Meadow Loop, Alderfer/Three Sisters Medley, Apex Loop Trail, Red Rocks/Dakota Ridge Loop, and High Line Canal Trail. Of this group, I see no reason why anyone uses the overworked Apex Trail, which is in serious need of trail reconstruction. Nonetheless, it is included here due to its popularity. Trails seeing increased trail runner activity are the Green Mountain Loop, Lair to Pence Connector Trail, Mount Falcon Loop, and Mount Galbraith Loop.

Strangely enough, the highest-quality trails are not necessarily the most popular. The Colorado/Green Mountain Trails system is perhaps the finest run in the Denver area, but requires at least a forty-mile drive for most Denver residents. The relatively short Meyer Ranch Loop and

Shadow Mountain Loop trails are in excellent condition and among my favorites, but also require a modest drive from Denver.

If buying a park pass is no concern, then try the Carpenter Peak Trail and Roxborough Park Medley, both located in Roxborough Park to the southwest of Denver. The park's trail maintenance is excellent, though they have a bad habit of closing the park gates after hours, so call them (see the Appendix) for the park's closing hours, which vary by season. The Castlewood Canyon Loop also requires a park pass and is subject to park closure, but is a great off-season run with a wide variety of terrain.

A special note on mountain bikers: there are lots of them, so get used to co-habiting trails. Just because they are on bikes and you are not, do not assume that mountain bikers go faster than runners. On the contrary, runners hold a clear edge on hilly courses, and can easily over-take bikers. Though I take a particularly fiendish pleasure in quietly running up behind mountain bikers who think they are alone and scaring them out of their skins, it is generally better to announce your presence while still some yards away. In the Denver area, mountain bikers are especially common on the Apex, White Ranch, Alderfer, Colorado, Elk Meadow, Green Mountain, Lair to Pence, Mount Falcon, Red Rocks, Plymouth Mountain, and Red Mesa trails - in short, pretty much anywhere they are allowed. The Jefferson County Open Space park system is experimenting with building and designating new trails for foot travel only. The Mount Galbraith Loop (opened in 2001) was specifically constructed with the intent that it will be used only by trail runners, hikers, and the like - bicycles are prohibited.

Apex Loop 20

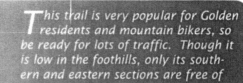

*Near Bonanza and
Grubstake Loop.*

*T*his trail is very popular for Golden residents and mountain bikers, so be ready for lots of traffic. Though it is low in the foothills, only its southern and eastern sections are free of snow through the winter, with the north facing sections of the Grubstake Loop Trail being buried until mid-April. In summer, temperatures are likely to be very hot on the trail, so plan for an early start.

Rating

Moderate

Location: Just southwest of the City of Golden
Distance/Type: 5.1 miles loop
Running Time: 1.0 hours
Starting Elevation: 6,160 feet
Elevation Gain: 1,340 feet
Best Season: March through November
Jurisdiction: Jefferson County Open Space
Map(s): *Trails Illustrated # 100*
Permits/Fees: None

Grade: Steep in parts of the Apex and Sluicebox Trails, with an eight degree average angle of ascent. The trail is generally well-maintained, but watch out for some loose rocks, especially while descending the Pick 'N Sledge Trail on the return.

Getting There: From the intersection of I-70 and C-470, travel 0.9 miles west on I-70 to the Morrison exit (Exit 259). Turn right off this exit and head north on Route 40 for 0.9 miles. This brings you to the entrance of the Heritage Square shopping area. Turn left to enter the Heritage Square access road, and then

Mileage *GO*

0.0 Head west on Apex Trail.
1.4 Turn north onto Sluicebox Trail.
2.1 Join Grubstake Loop. Head North.
3.1 Bear east and south on Grubstake Loop.
3.7 Turn east on Pick 'N Sledge Trail.
4.6 Rejoin Apex Trail. Head east.
5.1 Arrive at parking lot.

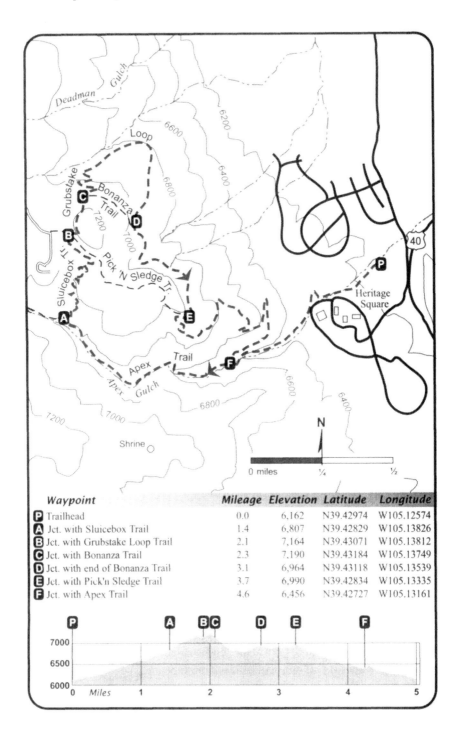

Waypoint	Mileage	Elevation	Latitude	Longitude
P Trailhead	0.0	6,162	N39.42974	W105.12574
A Jct. with Sluicebox Trail	1.4	6,807	N39.42829	W105.13826
B Jct. with Grubstake Loop Trail	2.1	7,164	N39.43071	W105.13812
C Jct. with Bonanza Trail	2.3	7,190	N39.43184	W105.13749
D Jct. with end of Bonanza Trail	3.1	6,964	N39.43118	W105.13539
E Jct. with Pick'n Sledge Trail	3.7	6,990	N39.42834	W105.13335
F Jct. with Apex Trail	4.6	6,456	N39.42727	W105.13161

immediately turn right to enter a large parking area. Park on the north side of the large lot, near the trail head.

The Route Description

Leave the trailhead at mile 0.0 (6160) on the north side of the parking lot and immediately turn left at the trailhead sign. After a few yards, another access trail will merge in from another parking area on the left. The trail turns right and crosses a bridge. After a few yards, turn left at the Apex Trail sign. The trail heads straight west into the foothills, rising gradually. Just after a short rocky section, the Pick 'N Sledge Trail will drop down from the right. Continue on the Apex Trail. It continues to ascend steadily over slightly rocky terrain. Though generally open to the sun, a few more trees will appear. At mile 1.4 (6810), the Sluicebox Trail will split off to the right. Take the Sluicebox Trail, heading roughly north. The trail ascends steeply through a series of switchbacks. Near the top, a housing area will appear on the left in an open area, while a large antenna will appear dead ahead through the trees.

You will come to a three-way junction at mile 2.1 (7160). Ignore the access trail that comes in from the housing division to the left (west). Instead, pass the Pick 'N Sledge Trail that branches off to the right, taking instead the Grubstake Loop Trail, which is the second trail on the right. After all the climbing, it is time for some fun. Cruise through wooded hillsides on hard pack trail as the Grubstake Loop Trail passes the Bonanza Trail Junction at mile 2.3 (7190), drops through switchbacks into a streambed, and then curls around to the east and then the south, affording great views of Golden to the north and the western suburbs of Denver. The far end of the Bonanza Trail merges in from the right at mile 3.1 (6960). Continue straight ahead on the Grubstake Loop, mostly through open meadows. At mile 3.7, (6990), the Pick 'N Sledge Trail merges in on the right. Continue ahead, dropping rapidly on great single track trail to a junction with the Apex Trail at mile 4.6 (6460). Turn left onto the Apex Trail and run back down to the trailhead at mile 5.1 (6160). Don't forget to return to your car in the lower parking lot. You may inadvertently return to the upper lot, so be sure to continue left down the trail for an extra hundred yards.

21 Golden Gate Canyon Loop

A beautifully scenic run, not only because of the wildlife you are bound to encounter, but the aspen, wildflowers and peak views are spectacular as well. Do be careful though as the trail consistency changes constantly. Running this trail requires vigilance.

Near the highpoint of the Mountain Lion Trail.

Rating

Moderate

Mileage

0.0 Head north on Burro Trail.
0.7 Turn northeast on Mt. Lion Trail.
1.4 Bear north on Mt. Lion Trail.
2.7 Take a hard left at 3-way Mt. Lion Trail junction.
4.4 Continue southeast on Mt. Lion Trail.
6.3 Head southwest through Nott parking lot.
7.4 Turn south on Burro Trail.
8.1 Arrive back at parking lot.

Location: 16.0 miles northwest of Golden
Distance/Type: 8.1 miles loop
Running Time: 2.0 hours
Starting Elevation: 7,840 feet
Elevation Gain: 1,870 feet
Best Season: May through October
Jurisdiction: Colorado State Park (Golden Gate Canyon State Park)
Map(s): *Trails Illustrated # 100*
Permits/Fees: $5 daily pass

Grade: Rolling, with a number of short, steep ascents. The trail is an odd mixture of excellent, smooth single track surface and rough, rutted track. This can be a surprisingly difficult run.

Getting There: From the junction of C-470 and I-70, take the Route 6 turnoff going northbound and follow it 3.8 miles to the junction of Routes 93, 6, and 58. From that intersection, take Route 93 north for 1.3 miles and turn left onto Golden Gate Canyon Road. Follow this road west for 12.25 miles to the entrance to the Golden Gate Canyon Park, turning off to the right to purchase a day pass at a roadside kiosk. Then continue down the road 100 yards, turning right

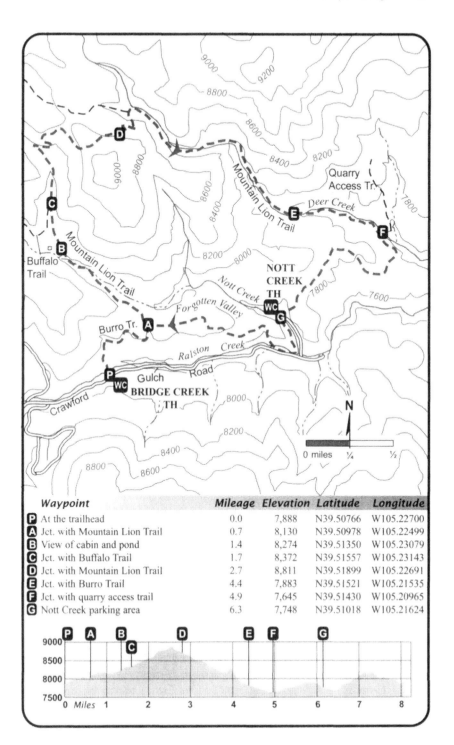

Waypoint		Mileage	Elevation	Latitude	Longitude
P	At the trailhead	0.0	7,888	N39.50766	W105.22700
A	Jct. with Mountain Lion Trail	0.7	8,130	N39.50978	W105.22499
B	View of cabin and pond	1.4	8,274	N39.51350	W105.23079
C	Jct. with Buffalo Trail	1.7	8,372	N39.51557	W105.23143
D	Jct. with Mountain Lion Trail	2.7	8,811	N39.51899	W105.22691
E	Jct. with Burro Trail	4.4	7,883	N39.51521	W105.21535
F	Jct. with quarry access trail	4.9	7,645	N39.51430	W105.20965
G	Nott Creek parking area	6.3	7,748	N39.51018	W105.21624

onto Crawford Gulch Road. Follow this road 2.2 miles and park on the left side of the road next to the bathroom. You are at the Bridge Creek trailhead.

The Route Description

From the Bridge Creek trailhead, head north out of the parking lot on the Burro Trail and immediately cross a bridge over Ralston Creek. Turn sharply left and follow the switch backing trail as it ascends continuously over a good quality single track surface to a junction with the Mountain Lion Trail at mile 0.7 (8130). At the junction, turn left onto the Mountain Lion Trail, which you will follow in a clockwise loop until returning to this junction. The trail is marked with a mountain lion's paw print. The trail soon widens into double track that is both rutted and sandy in places, but certainly negotiable. Pass a small pond and cabin as well as the Buffalo Trail at mile 1.4 (8270). Turn right at another junction with the Buffalo Trail at mile 1.7 (8370) in order to stay on the Mountain Lion Trail. The trail climbs steeply at times on a rough scree surface to a three-way junction at mile 2.7 (8810). This is an odd junction, since all three trails are marked as being the Mountain Lion Trail.

You can go straight ahead, which shortly brings you to the Burro Trail and a shorter run back to the trailhead. However, if you want a more adventurous run, turn hard left and follow the Mountain Lion Trail. This route gradually descends through a series of very rocky switchbacks in a pine forest on a generally north and then easterly heading. The trail stays in the vicinity of Deer Creek as the angle of descent lessens. During summer, vegetation can obscure rocks in the trail, so run carefully near the creek. Be prepared for lots of stream crossings - there are nine log bridges and two plank bridges in this section.

Ignore a junction with the Burro Trail at mile 4.4 (7880), which drops in from the right, and forge ahead on the Mountain Lion Trail until you come to a junction with a quarry access trail at mile 4.9 (7650). Turn right here, cross a plank bridge, and ascend over several ridges to an overlook of the Crawford Gulch Road. From here, drop to the Nott Creek Trailhead at mile 6.3 (7750), where another bathroom is located. Run through the Nott Creek parking lot and pick up the Mountain Lion Trail on its far side. After a few hundred yards, the trail ascends quite steeply heading southwest, and continues to climb until it reaches a junction with the Burro Trail at mile 7.4 (8130). Turn left onto the Burro Trail and follow it down good single track to the trailhead. Depending on foliage conditions, the final few yards may be in view of the parking area, so show good form before you cross the bridge and finish the run at mile 8.1 (7890).

White Ranch Loop 22

Despite its rough surface, this trail is surprisingly popular with mountain bikers, so look out for them on the downhill sections. Also, the route described here covers only a portion of the park. You can continue into its northern extremities on the Rawhide Trail to add another 4.5 miles and 1,000 vertical feet to the route. The route moves in and out of trees and a gorgeous meadow over much it its distance.

Running along the Belcher Hill Trail.

Location: 4.0 miles northwest of Golden
Distance/Type: 7.8 miles loop
Running Time: 1.5 hours
Starting Elevation: 6,170 feet
Elevation Gain: 1,630 feet
Best Season: March through November
Jurisdiction: Jefferson County Open Space (White Ranch Park)
Map(s): *Trails Illustrated # 100*
Permits/Fees: None

Grade: An eight degree average angle of ascent, though the very rocky surface during the first two miles makes it seem harder.

Getting There: From the junction of C-470 and I-70, take the Route 6 turnoff going northbound and follow it 3.8 miles to the junction of Routes 93, 6, and 58. From that intersection, take Route 93 north for 3.0 miles and turn left onto 56th Avenue. Follow it west for 1.1 miles, and turn right into the parking lot.

Rating

Moderate

Mileage

0.0 Take Belcher Hill Trail north.
1.8 Turn north onto Longhorn Trail.
2.2 Head west on Shrothorn Trail.
3.4 Bear west on Longhorn Trail.
4.5 Go south on Sawmill Trail.
5.1 Turn southeast on Belcher Hill Trail.
7.8 Arrive at parking lot.

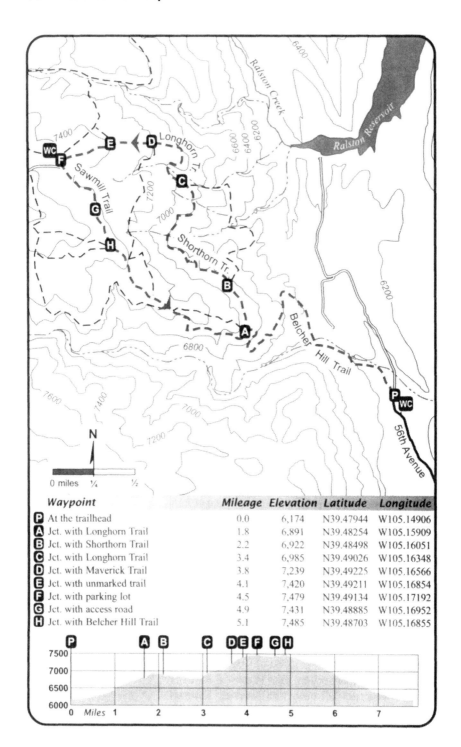

Waypoint	Mileage	Elevation	Latitude	Longitude
P At the trailhead	0.0	6,174	N39.47944	W105.14906
A Jct. with Longhorn Trail	1.8	6,891	N39.48254	W105.15909
B Jct. with Shorthorn Trail	2.2	6,922	N39.48498	W105.16051
C Jct. with Longhorn Trail	3.4	6,985	N39.49026	W105.16348
D Jct. with Maverick Trail	3.8	7,239	N39.49225	W105.16566
E Jct. with unmarked trail	4.1	7,420	N39.49211	W105.16854
F Jct. with parking lot	4.5	7,479	N39.49134	W105.17192
G Jct. with access road	4.9	7,431	N39.48885	W105.16952
H Jct. with Belcher Hill Trail	5.1	7,485	N39.48703	W105.16855

View of North Table Mountain from the Belcher Hill Trail.

The Route Description

Take the Belcher Hill Trail north out of the parking lot, which skirts an expensive subdivision before heading steeply uphill through rough terrain. Be warned: the Belcher Trail turns into a water slide when wet. Turn right at mile 1.8 (6890) onto the Longhorn Trail, and stay on this rough trail until you reach a junction at mile 2.2 (6920) with the Shorthorn Trail. Be sure to turn left onto the Shorthorn Trail here, since the trail grade and surface is much better on the Shorthorn Trail. The Longhorn Trail reappears and merges in from the right at mile 3.4 (6990), after which the combined trails are called the Longhorn Trail.

The Maverick Trail splits away to the left at mile 3.8 (7240); ignore it and stay right to remain on the Longhorn Trail. Ignore an unmarked turnoff at mile 4.1 (7420) and continue straight ahead. You will shortly pass a bathroom and paddock before arriving at a parking lot at mile 4.5 (7480). Run through the parking lot, cross a road heading south, and take the Sawmill Trail. The trail leads through a gorgeous meadow before merging into a wide, well-graded access road at mile 4.9 (7430). Turn right onto this road and follow it until mile 5.1 (7490), where there is a four-way junction. Turn left to access the Belcher Hill Trail. Follow it downhill back to the trailhead, ignoring numerous side trails branching off at various points. The traction can be loose in this area, so run carefully. The trailhead will appear at mile 7.8 (6170).

23 Alderfer/Three Sisters Medley

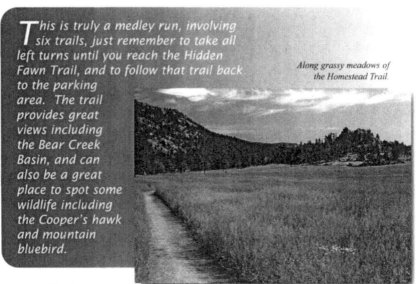

This is truly a medley run, involving six trails, just remember to take all left turns until you reach the Hidden Fawn Trail, and to follow that trail back to the parking area. The trail provides great views including the Bear Creek Basin, and can also be a great place to spot some wildlife including the Cooper's hawk and mountain bluebird.

Along grassy meadows of the Homestead Trail.

Rating

Moderate

Mileage

0.0 Start west out of the parking lot.
0.3 Head south on Evergreen Mountain Trail East.
3.2 Turn northwest on Wild Iris Loop.
3.9 Head northwest on Homestead Trail.
4.2 Go east on Silver Fox Trail.
4.5 Turn north on Sisters Trail.
5.3 Head south on Hidden Fawn Trail.
5.9 Arrive back at parking lot.

Location: Just south of Evergreen
Distance/Type: 5.9 miles medley
Running Time: 1.25 hours
Starting Elevation: 7,480 feet
Elevation Gain: 870 feet
Best Season: April through October
Jurisdiction: Jefferson County Open Space (Alderfer/Three Sisters Park)
Map(s): *Trails Illustrated # 100*
Permits/Fees: None

Grade: Moderate, with a 5 degree average angle of ascent. The trail is well-maintained, with few rocks, except on the Sisters Trail; this trail requires careful foot placement through large boulders and rocky steps.

Getting There: From the intersection of C-470 and Route 285, travel 13.7 miles west on Route 285 until you reach Conifer, where you take Route 73 north for 8.0 miles to a traffic light. Turn left onto Buffalo Park Road and drive 1.3 miles to reach the parking lot, which will be on the right. This trailhead can also be

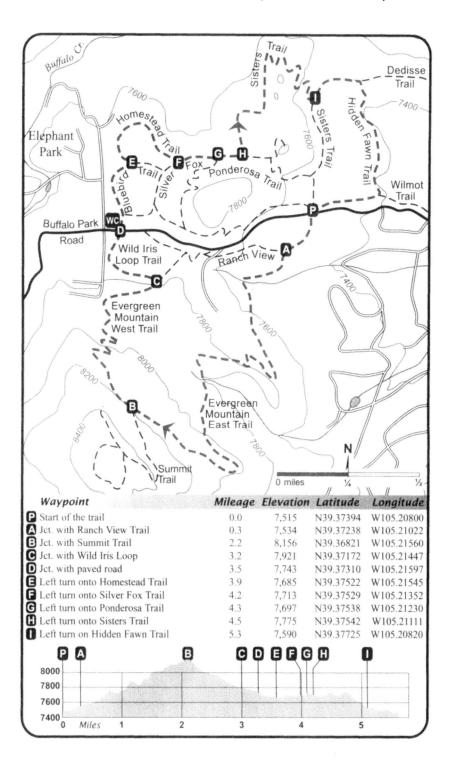

Waypoint		Mileage	Elevation	Latitude	Longitude
P	Start of the trail	0.0	7,515	N39.37394	W105.20800
A	Jct. with Ranch View Trail	0.3	7,534	N39.37238	W105.21022
B	Jct. with Summit Trail	2.2	8,156	N39.36821	W105.21560
C	Jct. with Wild Iris Loop	3.2	7,921	N39.37172	W105.21447
D	Jct. with paved road	3.5	7,743	N39.37310	W105.21597
E	Left turn onto Homestead Trail	3.9	7,685	N39.37522	W105.21545
F	Left turn onto Silver Fox Trail	4.2	7,713	N39.37529	W105.21352
G	Left turn onto Ponderosa Trail	4.3	7,697	N39.37538	W105.21230
H	Left turn onto Sisters Trail	4.5	7,775	N39.37542	W105.21111
I	Left turn on Hidden Fawn Trail	5.3	7,590	N39.37725	W105.20820

reached from the north. The alternative directions are, from the intersection of C-470 and Interstate 70, travel 7.9 miles west on Interstate 70
to exit 252, which is the Evergreen Parkway exit. Take Route 74 south
for 7.4 miles until you reach the town of Evergreen. Turn right onto
Route 73, and travel 0.6 miles to the turnoff onto the Buffalo Park Road
that was previously mentioned.

The Route Description

From the parking lot, cross Buffalo Park Road and proceed straight
ahead on the Evergreen Mountain Trail. This is a gently rolling, wide
dirt path. At mile 0.3 (7590) turn left at the junction with the Ranch
View Trail to keep you on the Evergreen Mountain Trail East. The trail
ascends continually through increasingly thick pine forest, passing an
overlook on the left that affords great views of several lower Front
Range summits to the east. Pass the Summit Trail at mile 2.2 (7530),
which cuts off to the left. If you want extra mileage, take this trail for
a 1.4 mile loop that will take you back to the main trail after a 170 foot
elevation gain. Otherwise, continue down the Evergreen Mountain
Trail West on the well-groomed trail.

Turn left at mile 3.2 (8160) onto the Wild Iris Loop, which cuts
through an open field, leading you back to the Buffalo Park Road at
mile 3.5 (7920) and a parking area on the far side. There are bathroom
facilities here. From the parking lot, turn left onto the Bluebird Trail,
which heads north toward a small rock formation. Just before the rock
formation at mile 3.9 (7740), turn left onto the Homestead Trail, which
re-enters a sparse pine forest area and curls around to the north and then
east. Turn left onto the Silver Fox Trail at mile 4.2 (7690). Turn left yet
again at mile 4.3 (7710) onto the Ponderosa Trail. The grade begins to
slightly become steep, but you won't be on this trail long enough to feel
the change.

Turn left onto the Sisters Trail at mile 4.5 (7700). The trail soon
ascends through open pine forests. Be careful of your footing in this
area. There are many large boulders and rocky steps that continue up
over a ridgeline and back down through a series of switchbacks as the
trail meanders to the east. Stop at the ridgeline for views in several
directions. After descending from the ridgeline, turn right onto the
Hidden Fawn Trail at mile 5.3 (7780), which you will follow generally
downhill back to the parking lot. Ignore side trails for the Dedisse Trail
and Wilmot Trail along the way. Arrive back at the parking lot at mile
5.9 (7520).

Bergen Peak Loop 24

View of Evergreen from the Too Long Trail.

Despite the difficult footing in places, there are great views in many spots that make this route well worth the effort. Just be sure to run this route in the recommended order, so you tackle most of the difficult footing during the ascent.

Rating

Moderate

Location: Just north of Evergreen
Distance/Type: 8.2 miles loop
Running Time: 1.5 hours
Starting Elevation: 7,775 feet
Elevation Gain: 1,570 feet
Best Season: April through October
Jurisdiction: Jefferson County Open Space (Elk Meadow Park), Denver Mountain Park
Map(s): *Trails Illustrated # 100*
Permits/Fees: None

Grade: An average angle of ascent of seven degrees, but it seems harder when you throw in the roots, small rocks, medium rocks, really big rocks, and pea gravel littering the Bergen Peak Trail.

Getting There: From the junction of C-470 and I-70, travel west on I-70 to the Evergreen Parkway exit (Exit 252). Take the Parkway south for 5.4 miles to Stagecoach Boulevard. Turn right onto Stagecoach, which takes you west along the south edge of Elk Meadow Park for 1.2 miles, where there is a parking area on the right side of the road.

Mileage *GO*

0.0 Head northeast out of the parking lot.
0.3 Go west on Meadow View Trail.
0.9 Bear west on Bergen Peak Trail.
3.7 Head east on Too Long Trail.
6.0 Go south on Mountain View Trail.
7.9 Head south and west on Meadow View Trail.
8.2 Arrive back at parking lot.

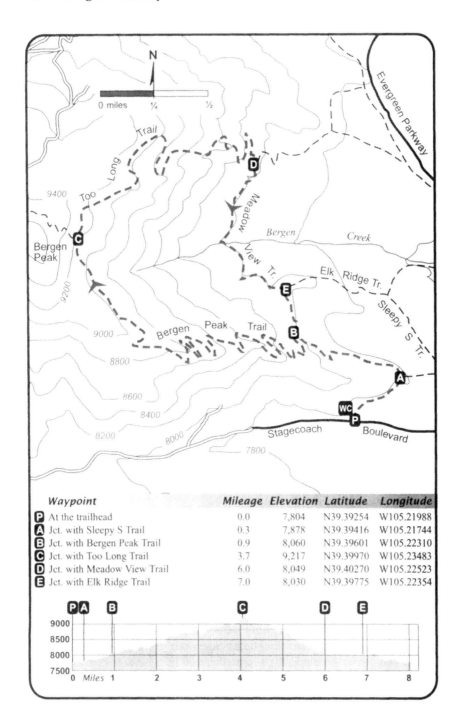

Waypoint	Mileage	Elevation	Latitude	Longitude
P At the trailhead	0.0	7,804	N39.39254	W105.21988
A Jct. with Sleepy S Trail	0.3	7,878	N39.39416	W105.21744
B Jct. with Bergen Peak Trail	0.9	8,060	N39.39601	W105.22310
C Jct. with Too Long Trail	3.7	9,217	N39.39970	W105.23483
D Jct. with Meadow View Trail	6.0	8,049	N39.40270	W105.22523
E Jct. with Elk Ridge Trail	7.0	8,030	N39.39775	W105.22354

The Route Description

From the trailhead, take the Meadow View Trail to the north, passing to the right of the bathrooms. At mile 0.3 (7880) junction with the Sleepy S Trail, stay to the left to remain on the Meadow View Trail. The trail now heads gradually uphill and west through pine forests to a trail junction at mile 0.9 (8060), where you turn left onto the Bergen Peak Trail. This is where the going gets interesting, with an alternating smooth surface and "can we make it any harder" conditions, featuring roots, embedded rocks and pea gravel. Several views will open up to the south, which may be worth a rest and a look.

The Bergen Peak Trail turns hard left at mile 3.7 (9220) and continues to the summit of Bergen Peak. Instead, go straight ahead on

Trailhead for the Meadow View Trail.
(courtesy Linda Grey)

the Too Long Trail. The trail surface soon becomes much easier, providing for a generally good descent through pine forests to a junction with the Meadow View Trail at mile 6.0 (8050). Turn right (south) onto the Meadow View Trail. There is generally good-to-excellent footing in this area, as well as gently rolling terrain - great running conditions! Blow by the Elk Ridge Trail, which splits off to the left at mile 7.0 (8030) and continue past the Bergen Peak Trail at mile 7.3 (8060) until you reach a junction with the Sleepy S Trail at mile 7.9 (7880). Turn right here to remain on the Meadow View Trail, and run down the short downhill remaining to take you back to the parking lot at mile 8.2 (7800).

25 Buck Gulch Loop

The uphill portion of this run is no joke, since there are hardly any truly flat sections where you can catch your breath. If you can ignore the rasp of your own tortured breathing, feel free to take in the excellent view of surrounding peaks and valleys.

Bikers along the Skipper Trail.

Rating

Moderate

Mileage

0.0 Head west on Narrow Gauge Trail.
0.4 Go south on North Fork View Trail/Buck Gulch Trail.
3.2 Turn east on Skipper Trail.
4.6 Go north on Strawberry Jack Trail.
6.8 Continue north on Buck Gulch Trail.
7.2 Head east on Narrow Gauge Trail.
7.6 Arrive at parking lot.

Location: 29.0 miles west of C-470
Distance/Type: 7.6 miles loop
Running Time: 1.5 hours
Starting Elevation: 6,860 feet
Elevation Gain: 1,220 feet
Best Season: March through November
Jurisdiction: Jefferson County Park (Pine Valley Ranch Park), Pike National Forest
Map(s): *Trails Illustrated # 105*
Permits/Fees: None

Grade: The trail designer conveniently packed nearly all of the vertical gain into a 2.4-mile stretch between mile 0.8 and mile 3.2, so you can agonize through a continuous ten-degree angle of ascent in one fun-filled segment. Once you crawl to the top, the rest of the run is a breeze, with a packed sand base underfoot.

Getting There: From the intersection of C-470 and Route 285, drive west on Route 285 for 20.0 miles until you reach Pine Junction. Turn left onto Pine Valley Road and drive south for 5.7 miles. Turn right onto Crystal Lake Road and drive 1.2 miles until you reach a multi-tiered parking area. Park in the lower parking lot.

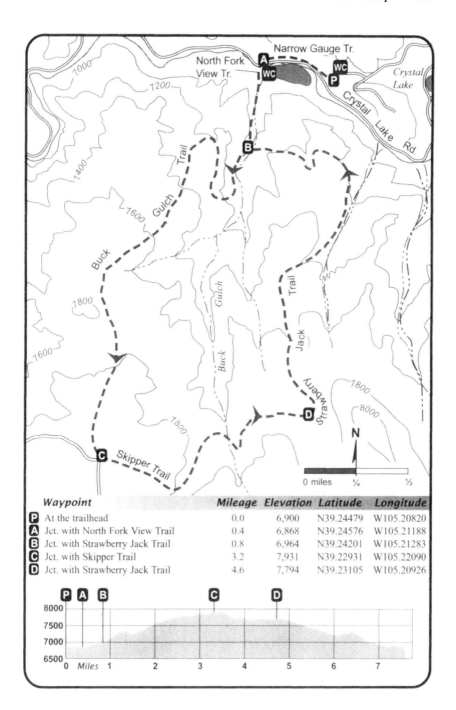

Waypoint	Mileage	Elevation	Latitude	Longitude
P At the trailhead	0.0	6,900	N39.24479	W105.20820
A Jct. with North Fork View Trail	0.4	6,868	N39.24576	W105.21188
B Jct. with Strawberry Jack Trail	0.8	6,964	N39.24201	W105.21283
C Jct. with Skipper Trail	3.2	7,931	N39.22931	W105.22090
D Jct. with Strawberry Jack Trail	4.6	7,794	N39.23105	W105.20926

The Route Description

Pass to the right of the bathrooms at the trailhead and follow the Narrow Gauge Trail until mile 0.4 (6870), where you turn left onto the North Fork View Trail, immediately crossing a bridge and passing to the right of yet more bathrooms. Pick up the Buck Gulch Trail here, which heads straight away from the bridge and into the trees. At mile 0.8 (6960), stay to the right at a junction with the Strawberry Jack Trail in order to remain on the Buck Gulch Trail. The angle of ascent steepens dramatically here and stays that way until just before mile 3.2 (7930), where you turn left onto the Skipper Trail just after a notice board. Follow this pleasantly flat trail until mile 4.6 (7790), where there is a four-way junction. Turn left here to pick up the Strawberry Jack Trail, and follow it back downhill to the earlier junction with the Buck Gulch Trail at mile 6.8 (6960). From there, it is a quick cruise back to the bridge crossing, followed by a right turn onto the Narrow Gauge Trail that brings you back to the parking lot at mile 7.6 (6900).

Colorado/Green Mountain Trails 26

Heading west from the Colorado Trail.

All things considered, this is the finest run in the Denver area. The trail rolls over a seemingly endless series of low, rolling hills. Though forest fires have ravaged much of this area, it has also eliminated much of the underbrush, resulting in excellent views. The only problem is that mountain bikers love this route too, and enjoy reaching warp speeds on the straighter sections. Consequently, a better running time is on weekdays, when the crowds are smaller.

Location: 35.0 miles west of C-470
Distance/Type: 13.9 miles trail
Running Time: 3.0 hours
Starting Elevation: 7,690 feet
Elevation Gain: 1,880 feet
Best Season: May through October
Jurisdiction: Pike National Forest
Map(s): *Trails Illustrated # 135*
Permits/Fees: None

Grade: Fabulous rolling hills on a packed sandy base. Though there is almost 2,000 feet of vertical gain, it is so spread out that you hardly notice it.

Getting There: From the intersection of C-470 and Route 285, drive west on Route 285 for 20.0 miles until you reach Pine Junction. Turn left onto Pine Valley Road and drive south for 13.1 miles. Turn right onto Route 550, drive for 1.5 miles, and turn right into the Shinglemill Trail parking area.

Rating — Difficult

Classics

Mileage GO

0.0 Head south on Shinglemill Trail.
0.2 Go south and west on Colorado Trail.
5.9 Turn south on Green Mountain Trail.
9.3 Rejoin Colorado Trail. Head east.
13.7 Go north on Shinglemill Trail.
13.9 Arrive at parking lot.

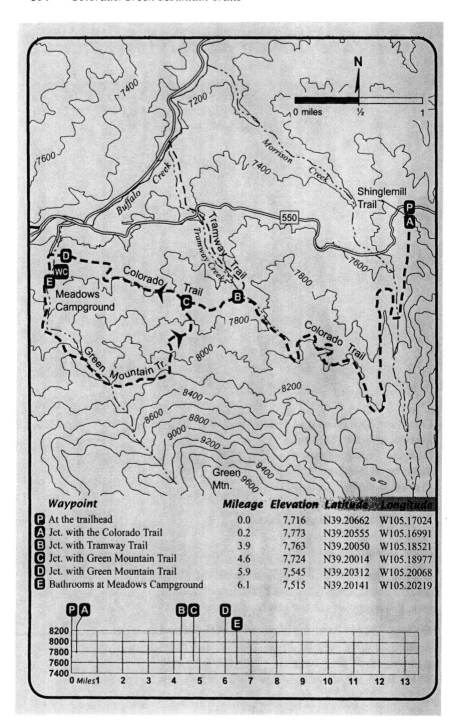

Waypoint	Mileage	Elevation	Latitude	Longitude
P At the trailhead	0.0	7,716	N39.20662	W105.17024
A Jct. with the Colorado Trail	0.2	7,773	N39.20555	W105.16991
B Jct. with Tramway Trail	3.9	7,763	N39.20050	W105.18521
C Jct. with Green Mountain Trail	4.6	7,724	N39.20014	W105.18977
D Jct. with Green Mountain Trail	5.9	7,545	N39.20312	W105.20068
E Bathrooms at Meadows Campground	6.1	7,515	N39.20141	W105.20219

The Route Description

Head south from the parking lot, crossing Route 550 to access the Shinglemill Trail. This is an access trail that will bring you to the Colorado Trail at mile 0.2 (7770). Turn right onto the Colorado Trail and stay on it through miles of pleasant rolling hills (some a tad burnt from recent fires). Remain on the Colorado Trail at mile 3.9 (7760), where the Tramway Trail branches off to the right, and at mile 4.6 (7720), where the Green Mountain Trail splits off to the left. Finally leave the Colorado Trail at mile 5.9 (7550), turning left onto the Green Mountain Trail, which circles back in a counter-clockwise loop to the earlier junction with the Colorado Trail, which you will reach at mile 9.3 (7550). Shortly after beginning the Green Mountain Trail, you will pass just to the left of the Meadows Campground at mile 6.1 (7520), which contains a bathroom.

The miles will roll by as you continue back down the Colorado Trail. The earlier junction with the Tramway Trail will arrive at mile 10.0 (7760), and the junction with the Shinglemill Trail at mile 13.7 (7770). Be sure to turn left here, so you can arrive back at the Shinglemill trailhead at mile 13.9 (7720).

27 Elk Meadow Loop

*T*his excellent trail system is ideal for a week-day run. Especially since it is so popular with bikers, runners, hikers and dog walkers. But whenever you decide to go, you won't be disap-pointed.

Runner along the Meadow View Trail.

Rating

Easy

Classics

Mileage

0.0 Head north and east on Meadow View Trail.

0.3 Turn west on Meadow View Trail.

2.2 Bear east on Meadow View Trail.

3.0 Turn south on Painters Pause Trail.

4.1 Go west on Sleepy S Trail.

4.6 Continue south on Sleepy S Trail.

5.4 Rejoin Meadow View Trail.

5.7 Arrive at parking lot.

Location: Just north of Evergreen
Distance/Type: 5.7 miles loop
Running Time: 1.0 hours
Starting Elevation: 7,780 feet
Elevation Gain: 550 feet
Best Season: April through October
Jurisdiction: Jefferson County Open Space (Elk Meadow Park)
Map(s): *Trails Illustrated* # 100
Permits/Fees: None

Grade: Minimal, with a two degree average angle of ascent. The trail is well-maintained.

Getting There: From the junction of C-470 and I-70, travel west on I-70 to the Evergreen Parkway exit (Exit 252). Take the Parkway south for 5.4 miles to Stagecoach Boulevard. Turn right onto Stagecoach, which takes you west along the south edge of Elk Meadow Park for 1.2 miles, where there is a parking area on the right side of the road.

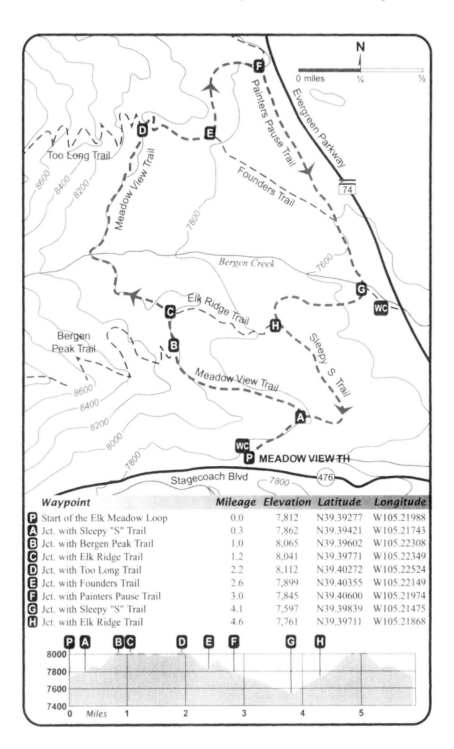

Waypoint		Mileage	Elevation	Latitude	Longitude
P	Start of the Elk Meadow Loop	0.0	7,812	N39.39277	W105.21988
A	Jct. with Sleepy "S" Trail	0.3	7,862	N39.39421	W105.21743
B	Jct. with Bergen Peak Trail	1.0	8,065	N39.39602	W105.22308
C	Jct. with Elk Ridge Trail	1.2	8,041	N39.39771	W105.22349
D	Jct. with Too Long Trail	2.2	8,112	N39.40272	W105.22524
E	Jct. with Founders Trail	2.6	7,899	N39.40355	W105.22149
F	Jct. with Painters Pause Trail	3.0	7,845	N39.40600	W105.21974
G	Jct. with Sleepy "S" Trail	4.1	7,597	N39.39839	W105.21475
H	Jct. with Elk Ridge Trail	4.6	7,761	N39.39711	W105.21868

The Route Description

The trail begins at the north side of the parking lot. From there, take the Meadow View Trail, which bends east and then north, ascending a small hill to a junction with the Sleepy "S" Trail at mile 0.3 (7860). Turn left to stay on the Meadow View Trail and run northwest through pine forest to the junction with Bergen Peak Trail, which branches off to the left at mile 1.0 (8070). Continue north to the next junction at mile 1.2 (8040), where the Elk Ridge Trail branches off to the right. Continue straight ahead (north) on the Meadow View Trail. Though the average angle of ascent is listed here as zero, the high point of the run, at 8,020 feet, is reached midway through this segment.

The Too Long Trail comes in from the left at mile 2.2 (8110). Stay on the Meadow View Trail as it turns right and drops into an open meadow. The Founders Trail splits off to the right at mile 2.6 (7900). Stay left on the Meadow View Trail and continue your descent towards the Evergreen Parkway. At mile 3.0 (7850), the Meadow View Trail terminates at a junction with the Painters Pause Trail, which parallels the Evergreen Parkway. Turn right and run south and downhill on the Painters Pause Trail through open meadow. At mile 3.7 (7640), the Founders Trail merges in from the right. Continue your descent south on the Painters Pause Trail.

Time to pay for the drop in elevation! Turn hard right onto the Sleepy "S" Trail at mile 4.1 (7600), just before reaching a parking area and bathrooms, and jog uphill over several water bars. Just to the west of the parking area, the trail splits in two. Take the right turn to stay on the Sleepy "S" Trail, which takes you south and up a steeper gradient. Stay left on the Sleepy "S" Trail at mile 4.6 (7760), where the Elk Ridge Trail departs on the left. The climbing is over at mile 5.4 (7850). Top out on a ridge line amongst pine trees. Turn left onto the Meadow View Trail and run downhill past the bathrooms and into the parking lot at mile 5.7 (7810). Time for another lap?

Green Mountain Loop 28

Near the Florida Trailhead.

This route is ideal because of its proximity to Denver, making it very convenient. However, there is no signage except at trailheads and no trees, which can make it hot and windswept. It can also be treacherous if it has just rained due to its clay soil. Watch out for mountain bikers, who like to travel this route at high speeds.

Rating

Moderate

Location: Southeast of the intersection of C-470 and I-70
Distance/Type: 6.9 miles loop
Running Time: 1.25 hours
Starting Elevation: 6,060 feet
Elevation Gain: 1,100 feet
Best Season: Nearly year-round
Jurisdiction: Lakewood Regional Park (Hayden Green Mountain Park)
Map(s): *Trails Illustrated # 100*
Permits/Fees: None

Grade: Easy at either end, with an overall average angle of ascent of three degrees. However, the ascent from the Florida Trailhead to the radio tower is at a seven degree angle of ascent. The trail is occasionally rocky during the same section. Also, look out for thick mud during the steep descent if it has rained recently.

Getting There: Take the Morrison Exit on C-470, go west 100 feet from the exit ramp, and turn north

GO

Mileage

0.0 Head east out of parking lot.
0.2 Go south on Green Mountain Trail.
2.0 Bear west at the 4-way junction.
3.6 Head northeast through the parking lot.
4.2 Go west at 3-way junction.
5.7 Turn southwest on Green Mountain Trail.
6.9 Arrive back at parking lot.

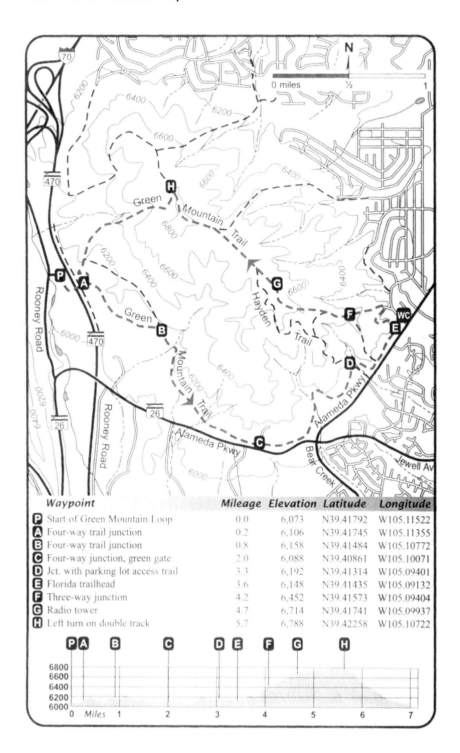

Waypoint		Mileage	Elevation	Latitude	Longitude
P	Start of Green Mountain Loop	0.0	6,073	N39.41792	W105.11522
A	Four-way trail junction	0.2	6,106	N39.41745	W105.11355
B	Four-way trail junction	0.8	6,158	N39.41484	W105.10772
C	Four-way junction, green gate	2.0	6,088	N39.40861	W105.10071
D	Jct. with parking lot access trail	3.3	6,192	N39.41314	W105.09401
E	Florida trailhead	3.6	6,148	N39.41435	W105.09132
F	Three-way junction	4.2	6,452	N39.41573	W105.09404
G	Radio tower	4.7	6,714	N39.41741	W105.09937
H	Left turn on double track	5.7	6,788	N39.42258	W105.10722

onto Rooney Road. Travel 2.4 miles north to a "T" intersection. Turn left onto Alameda Avenue and travel 0.4 miles, passing over C-470, to a right turn with no signage. Take the turn and continue north for 0.6 miles, paralleling C-470, to a right turn into the parking lot for the Rooney Trailhead. The park's name is the William Fredrick Hayden Green Mountain Park.

The Route Description

From the parking lot, take the paved path east over C-470. Immediately after crossing the bridge, at mile 0.2 (6110), you will have a choice of four trails. Take the first dirt trail to your right, which ignores a paved path to your right and two more dirt paths further to your left. The trail ascends on nice single track over several low ridges. The trail reaches a high point of 6,160 feet and then gradually curls around the south side of Green Mountain, paralleling Alameda Avenue. At mile 0.8 (6160), turn right at a four-way junction. At mile 2.0 (6090), go straight through a four-way intersection. Do not turn right at the green gate at this junction.

You will pass by the Utah trailhead, which is hidden on the right by a small hill. At mile 3.3 (6190), a trail will come up from the parking lot, cross the main trail, and continue uphill to the left. Ignore this trail and continue east around the mountain. You will soon pass the small hill, allowing a view of the Utah parking lot slightly behind you and to the right. The trail ascends slightly and tops out just to the right of a small fence. The Florida Trailhead is straight ahead. At mile 3.6 (6150), run straight through the parking area and take the trail commencing at its far (east) end. There is a temporary bathroom in this parking lot. The trail switchbacks up the side of Green Mountain (you are in clear view of the parking lot, so use good form!). The grade is steep and the footing is somewhat rocky.

At 4.2 miles (6450) turn left at a three-way junction. The trail curls over the top of the mountain, revealing wide vistas in all directions. Straight ahead is a radio tower. The double-track trail takes you straight to it. The trail veers away to the left at a three-way junction where you reach the radio tower at mile 4.7 (6710). Follow it up over a series of low ridges, passing the high point at 6,885 feet. Shortly thereafter at mile 5.7 (6790), the double-track turns hard left, while a fainter single-track forges on ahead. Turn left following the double-track road and descend steeply back to the trailhead. Be very careful in this area if it has rained recently, since the clay surface becomes very slick and sticks in thick slabs to your shoes. Finish the run by crossing over the highway and bearing right into the parking lot at mile 6.9 (6070).

29 Lair to Pence Connector

A very smooth and scenic run that includes a diverse geological landscape of forests, meadows and streams. Although this route is not meant for the novice runner due to the 2,150 feet of vertical ascent, one can easily turn around at any point and head back to the parking lot. It is an extremely popular route, especially with mountain bikers so be mindful of them. If running this route in the winter, be aware that dogs sometimes cross the frozen stream and can harass runners.

View from top of Pence Connector. (Gretchen Hanisch)

Rating

Difficult

GO

Mileage

0.0 Go west on Bear Creek Trail.
1.2 Head south on Bear Creek Trail.
4.3 Bear west on Bear Creek Trail.
4.5 Go south on Bear Creek Trail.
5.0 Continue south on Bear Creek Trail.
5.4 Head west on Bear Creek Trail.
6.1 Turnaround at Pence parking lot. Retrace route.
12.2 Arrive back at parking lot.

Location: 6.0 miles west of Morrison
Distance/Type: 12.2 miles trail
Running Time: 2.0 hours
Starting Elevation: 6,540 feet
Elevation Gain: 2,150 feet
Best Season: March through November
Jurisdiction: Jefferson County Open Space (Lair of the Bear), Denver Mountain Parks (Corwina, O'Fallon and Pence)
Map(s): *Trails Illustrated # 100*
Permits/Fees: None

Grade: A fabulous running trail with an average angle of ascent of seven degrees. The trail is relatively new, and so is generally smooth.

Getting There: From the Morrison exit on C-470, travel west on Route 8 for 5.1 miles. Turn left into the entrance of the Lair O' the Bear Park.

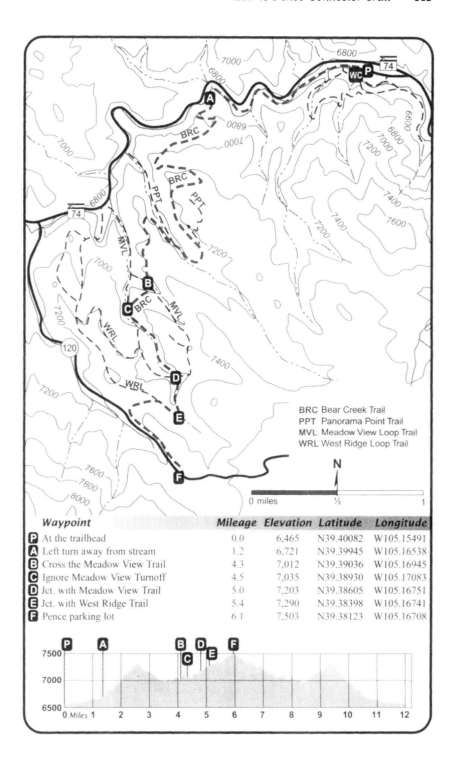

Waypoint	Mileage	Elevation	Latitude	Longitude
P At the trailhead	0.0	6,465	N39.40082	W105.15491
A Left turn away from stream	1.2	6,721	N39.39945	W105.16538
B Cross the Meadow View Trail	4.3	7,012	N39.39036	W105.16945
C Ignore Meadow View Turnoff	4.5	7,035	N39.38930	W105.17083
D Jct. with Meadow View Trail	5.0	7,203	N39.38605	W105.16751
E Jct. with West Ridge Trail	5.4	7,290	N39.38398	W105.16741
F Pence parking lot	6.1	7,503	N39.38123	W105.16708

BRC Bear Creek Trail
PPT Panorama Point Trail
MVL Meadow View Loop Trail
WRL West Ridge Loop Trail

The Route Description

From the west end of the parking lot, take the Bear Creek Trail, which you will follow for the entire route. This initial section is on wide double track trail, and stays to the left of a stream. At mile 1.2 (6720), continue to follow the Bear Creek Trail as it shrinks to single track and turns sharply left away from the stream and follows a series of switchbacks as the trail traverses up a forested hillside. The trail reaches a high point of ,7300 feet at about mile 2.8, where many people stop for a rest. The trail then drops slightly as it heads generally south to mile 4.3 (7010), where it crosses the Meadow View Trail. Continue on Bear Creek Trail, ignoring a sharp right turnoff at mile 4.5 (7040) where the Meadow View Trail branches away. The trail turns into double track, with weeds growing in the median. The irrepressible Meadow View Trail again merges in from the left at mile 5.0 (7200). Stay left at mile 5.4 (7290), where the West Ridge Trail branches away to the right. The trail narrows to single track as it rises over a final hump. Then cross a paved road to reach the Pence Park parking area at mile 6.1 (7500). Turn around and head back to the parking lot, which is located at mile 12.2 (6470).

Meyer Ranch Loop 30

At the Meyer Ranch trailhead.

This picturesque route includes forested areas full of aspen, and in the Spring and Summer an array of wildflowers are present including Columbines and Indian paintbrush. Due to the number of trails listed, just remember to take all right turns.

Rating

Easy

Location: 11.0 miles west of C-470, just off route 285

Distance/Type: 4.3 miles loop

Running Time: 1.0 hours

Starting Elevation: 7,880 feet

Elevation Gain: 880 feet

Best Season: April through October

Jurisdiction: Jefferson County Open Space (Meyer Ranch Park)

Map(s): *Trails Illustrated # 100*

Permits/Fees: None

Grade: Moderate, with a 5 degree average angle of ascent. The trail is well-maintained, with few rocks.

Getting There: From the junction of C-470 and Route 285, travel west on Route 285 for 10.8 miles. At this point, you will have just topped out on a small hill and started to descend into a short, open valley. Take the right turn at the sign marked "Meyer Open Space Ranch," loop under the highway, and park on the south side of South Turkey Creek Road, which branches off Route 285 at this point.

Mileage

GO

0.0 Take Owl's Perch Trail out of the parking lot.

0.4 Head west on Lodgepole Loop Trail.

1.1 Turn south on Sunny Aspen Trail.

1.4 Go south on Old Ski Run Trail.

3.3 Turn east on Sunny Aspen Trail.

4.1 Rejoin Owl's Perch Trail.

4.3 Arrive back at parking lot.

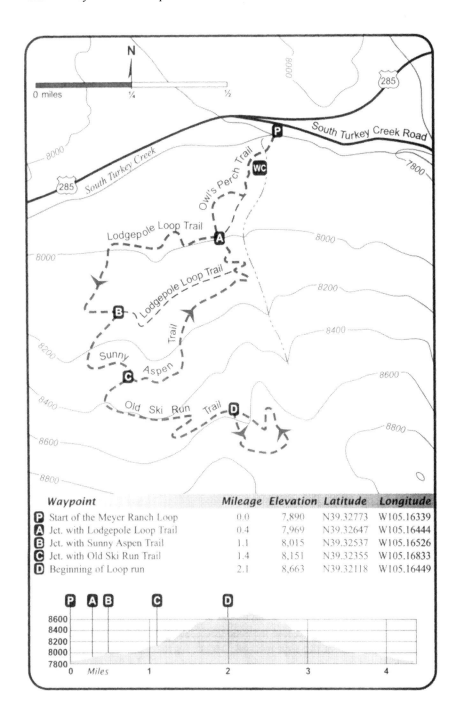

Waypoint	Mileage	Elevation	Latitude	Longitude
P Start of the Meyer Ranch Loop	0.0	7,890	N39.32773	W105.16339
A Jct. with Lodgepole Loop Trail	0.4	7,969	N39.32647	W105.16444
B Jct. with Sunny Aspen Trail	1.1	8,015	N39.32537	W105.16526
C Jct. with Old Ski Run Trail	1.4	8,151	N39.32355	W105.16833
D Beginning of Loop run	2.1	8,663	N39.32118	W105.16449

The Route Description

The trail begins at the southwest corner of the parking lot. From that point, take the Owl's Perch Trail up a short hill through a meadow, passing rest rooms on your left. At mile 0.2, turn right to follow the Owl's Perch Trail. This turn may not be marked. The trail will split shortly at a three-way junction. Take the right turn at mile 0.4 (7970) onto the Lodgepole Loop Trail. At a three-way junction at mile 1.1 (8020), take the Sunny Aspen Trail to the right. The angle of ascent steepens for a short stretch, terminating in front of a covered picnic table.

At a three-way junction at mile 1.4 (8150), turn left onto the Old Ski Run Trail, which continues uphill through a pine forest. At a three-way junction at mile 2.1 (8350) turn right and follow the Old Ski Run Trail around a loop, passing a side trail at mile 2.4 (8660) leading to an overlook. The ascent is over! Continue around the loop to return to the three-way junction. From the three-way junction of the Old Ski Run Trail, return rapidly downhill to the junction at the covered picnic table. At mile 3.3 (8015) take the Sunny Aspen Trail to the right, which takes you downhill through pine forests in a northeasterly direction. Descend along the eastern edge of the park boundary through a series of switch-backs until the Lodgepole Loop Trail joins from the left. Continue downhill to the Owl's Perch Trail at mile 4.1, where it joins from the left. Continue downhill, pass the bathrooms on your right, and follow the Owl's Perch Trail back through the meadow and into the parking lot at mile 4.3 (7890).

Benches along the route provide rest and view.

31 *Mount Falcon Loop*

Though this trail begins with a hard climb, the Parmalee Trail on the back side of the route is most rewarding, rolling through pine forests and open glades. Be sure to take the Turkey Trot Trail on the return and watch for great views of Red Rocks Park to the north.

Along the Parmalee Trail.

Rating

Difficult

GO

Mileage

0.0 Begin west on Castle Trail.
0.2 Turn northwest onto Turkey Trot Trail
1.9 head south on Castle Trail.
4.0 Turn south on Parmalee Trail.
6.2 Bear north on Meadows Trail.
6.6 Go east on Castle Trail.
8.4 Turn north on Turkey Trot Trail.
10.2 Arrive back at parking lot.

Location: 1.0 mile north of Route 285, just west of C-470
Distance/Type: 10.2 miles loop
Running Time: 2.0 hours
Starting Elevation: 6,020 feet
Elevation Gain: 2,250 feet
Best Season: April through October
Jurisdiction: Jefferson County Open Space (Mt. Falcon Park)
Map(s): *Trails Illustrated # 100*
Permits/Fees: None

Grade: A stiff initial climb, with a 10 degree average angle of ascent. The descent on the Castle Trail can be treacherous, due to a steep descent and some loose rocks.

Getting There: From the junction of C-470 and Route 285, travel west on Route 285 for 1.6 miles. Take the Morrison exit, turning north onto Route 8. Proceed north for 1.2 miles and take a left (west) turn onto Forest Avenue. Follow this road for 0.15 miles and turn right onto Vine Street. Follow Vine for 0.2 miles into the trailhead parking lot.

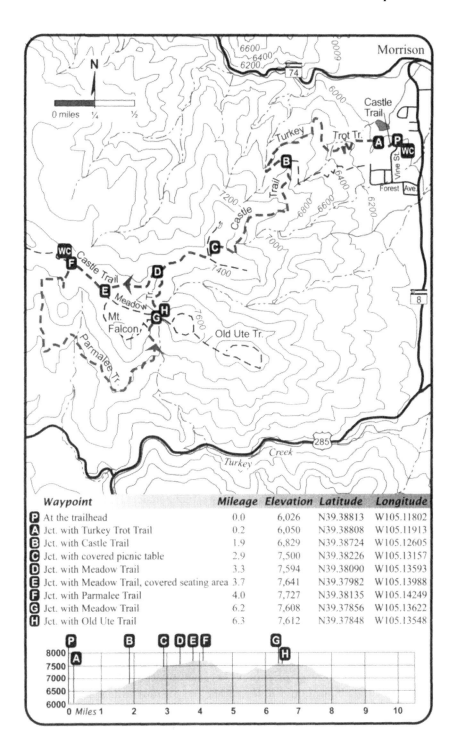

Waypoint	Mileage	Elevation	Latitude	Longitude
P At the trailhead	0.0	6,026	N39.38813	W105.11802
A Jct. with Turkey Trot Trail	0.2	6,050	N39.38808	W105.11913
B Jct. with Castle Trail	1.9	6,829	N39.38724	W105.12605
C Jct. with covered picnic table	2.9	7,500	N39.38226	W105.13157
D Jct. with Meadow Trail	3.3	7,594	N39.38090	W105.13593
E Jct. with Meadow Trail, covered seating area	3.7	7,641	N39.37982	W105.13988
F Jct. with Parmalee Trail	4.0	7,727	N39.38135	W105.14249
G Jct. with Meadow Trail	6.2	7,608	N39.37856	W105.13622
H Jct. with Old Ute Trail	6.3	7,612	N39.37848	W105.13548

The Route Description

Take the Castle Trail from the parking lot, passing to the right of the bathrooms and take the Turkey Trot Trail to the right at mile 0.2 (6050). This is a hikers only trail. Ascend steeply through a series of switchbacks on an open hillside. Once the trail reaches an initial ridge crest, the angle of ascent is much reduced as it plunges into a region of open glades. At mile 1.9 (6830), turn right at a "T" junction and follow the Castle Trail, ascending steeply to a fine overlook a few hundred yards up the trail. You are now sharing the path with mountain bikers, of whom those going downhill will be going at a great pace, so be vigilantly aware of your surroundings. This is a good time for a breather, because the trail launches into an unremittingly steep traverse to the southwest, terminating in a set of switchbacks that may be choked with snow until mid-Spring. Shortly after the switchbacks, the trail passes to the right of a covered picnic area at mile 5.4 (7500). Collapse here for a rest.

Follow the Castle Trail past the picnic area on a wide gravel service road. Ignore the Two-Dog Trail and Meadows Trail at mile 3.3 (7590), both of which merge in on the left side. There is a fine covered bench with a view at the junction with the Meadows Trail at mile 3.7 (7640). Stay on the Castle Trail, which bears somewhat to the right, until you reach the junction with the Parmalee Trail at mile 4.0 (7730), where a bathroom can also be found, and take a left turn. This entire area is a broad, open meadow rimmed with pine trees.

Here is where the fun begins. Plunge down a low-angle grade of single track trail that winds through a combination of meadows, glades, and pine forest, gradually curling to the south and then back east. At its further end, the trail gradually ascends through more open areas. The tread at the far end varies from loose rocks to loose sand, but is quite serviceable. At a junction with the Meadows Trail at mile 6.2 (7610), turn right and then stay on Meadows as the Old Ute Trail splits off to the right. Head north on Meadows until mile 6.6 (7590), where it rejoins the Castle Trail. Turn right (east) onto Castle Trail and follow it back downhill. This segment contains some loose rock, so it is easy to lose your footing and take a tumble here. Also, be aware that mountain bikers will almost certainly be struggling up this section, so give them plenty of leeway.

Turn left onto the Turkey Trot Trail at mile 8.4 (6830). Note that the trail junction is small and easy to miss, so stop at once when the junction sign appears and look for the trail. This is a luxurious descent, yielding great views of Red Rocks Park to the north as the trail winds back down through a series of loops and switchbacks. Push hard up a small grade just prior to the parking lot to finish at mile 10.2 (6030). Remember, the final half mile is in view of anyone at the parking lot, so show good form while you finish the run.

Mount Galbraith Loop 32

The Cedar Gulch Trail winds along the hillside.

Despite its short distance, this trail packs a punch. It ascends continuously for the first 1.3 miles, crosses a number of rocky ledges that require careful negotiation, and cuts across steep slopes in several spots. The trail surface is generally good, but be careful not to slip. Also, watch out for the stream crossing at the trailhead. There is no bridge at this time, and the stream can be difficult to cross during high water conditions.

Rating

Moderate

Location: 3.0 miles northwest of Golden
Distance/Type: 4.0 miles loop
Running Time: 1.0 hour
Starting Elevation: 6,280 feet
Elevation Gain: 1,010 feet
Best Season: March through November
Jurisdiction: Jefferson County Open Space (Mt. Galbraith Park)
Map(s): *Trails Illustrated # 100*
Permits/Fees: None

Grade: The trail has a nine degree average angle of ascent for the first 1.3 miles, after which the Mount Galbraith Loop Trail is much more tolerable. The trail crosses a number of rocky ledges, over which you should walk - not run.

Getting There: From the junction of C-470 and I-70, take the Route 6 turnoff going northbound and follow it 3.8 miles to the junction of Routes 93, 6, and 58. From that intersection, take Route 93 north for

Mileage

0.0 Start south on the Cedar Gulch Trail.
1.3 Turn southeast on Mount Galbraith Loop Trail.
2.7 Go north on Cedar Gulch Trail.
4.0 Arrive back at parking lot.

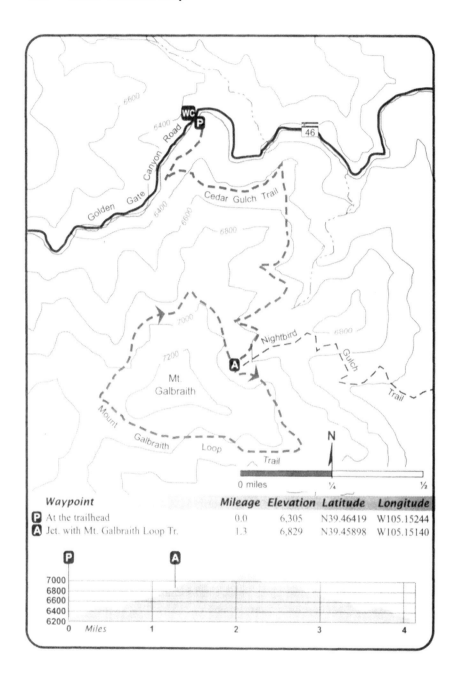

Waypoint	Mileage	Elevation	Latitude	Longitude
P At the trailhead	0.0	6,305	N39.46419	W105.15244
A Jct. with Mt. Galbraith Loop Tr.	1.3	6,829	N39.45898	W105.15140

1.3 miles and turn left onto Golden Gate Canyon Road. Follow this road west for 1.25 miles to the entrance of the Mount Galbraith Park, which will be on the left.

The Route Description

From the parking lot, take the Cedar Gulch Trail going southbound. Cross a stream at once and follow the trail as it stays to the east of the stream. The trail switchbacks after a few hundred yards and turns sharply east, then south, and then southwest. The trail crosses numerous mountain ridges during these perambulations. It is best to switch to walking as you pass over the rocky outcroppings that appear at the crest of every ridge. At mile 1.3 (6830), turn left at the junction with the Mount Galbraith Loop Trail. After a few feet, the Nightbird Gulch Trail will appear on the left. Continue on the Mount Galbraith Loop Trail as it enters a short stretch of pine forest and emerges onto an open field (where you can see and hear most of downtown Golden), and turns west along a bumpy ridge (from which you can see Green Mountain in the distance). Then cross the run's high point of 7,200 feet and turn northeast through pine trees as it completes the circuit of Mount Galbraith. Be particularly careful near the end of this segment, as the trail enters a rocky segment that is cut through a steep slope. There is also a short, sharp descent on rock stairs that demands a halt to all running.

Arrive back at the Cedar Gulch Trail and begin a pleasant descent back to the trailhead. Note that the upper stretches of this trail have a pronounced downhill slant to the right that is particularly noticeable during the descent. As usual, be careful while crossing all rock outcroppings. Cross the stream and arrive back at the trailhead at mile 4.0 (6310).

33 Red Rocks/Dakota Ridge Loop

*A*very scenic run with amazing views of Denver and Morrison as well as the red rock formations. The Dakota Ridge is quite rocky in places, so keep a slow pace. The Red Rocks Trail is much smoother. Expect mountain bikers on all segments of this trail as well as traffic noise along the northern and eastern segments of the trail, where major highways are located.

Hikers along the Dakota Ridge crest.

Rating

Moderate

Classics

Mileage *GO*

0.0 Start northeast out of the parking lot.
0.4 Turn south on Dakota Ridge Trail.
2.3 Bear west at Alameda Parkway junction.
3.1 Turn west and then north on Red Rocks Trail.
5.9 Arrive back at parking lot.

Location: 1.0 mile west of the C-470 and I-70 intersection.
Distance/Type: 5.9 miles loop
Running Time: 1.25 hours
Starting Elevation: 6,360 feet
Elevation Gain: 1,170 feet
Best Season: Nearly year-round
Jurisdiction: Jefferson County Open Space (Matthew/Winters Park)
Map(s): *Trails Illustrated # 100*
Permits/Fees: None

Grade: Moderate overall, though there are steep sections at the beginning of the route and just prior to the junction with the Morrison Slide Trail. The Dakota Ridge Trail is rocky in numerous places.

Getting There: From the junction of C-470 and I-70, travel I-70 westbound for 1.0 mile to the Morrison exit (Exit 259). Take the exit, turn left (south) and travel.0.25 miles to the entrance of the Matthews/Winters Park, which is on the right. If this parking lot is full, use the *Stegosaurus* lot across the road and slightly to the north.

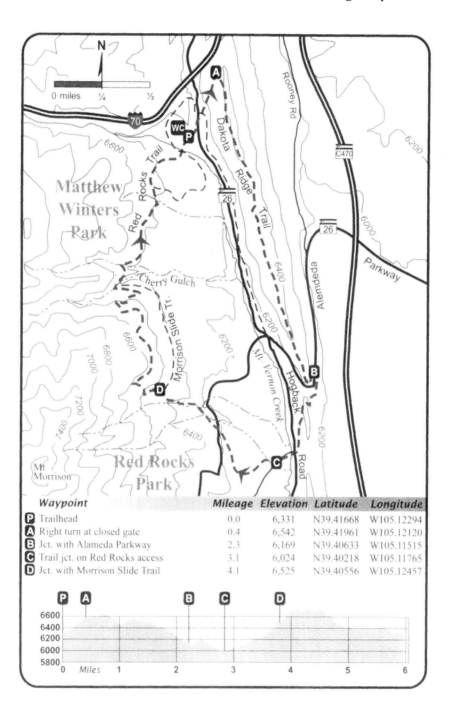

Waypoint		Mileage	Elevation	Latitude	Longitude
P	Trailhead	0.0	6,331	N39.41668	W105.12294
A	Right turn at closed gate	0.4	6,542	N39.41961	W105.12120
B	Jct. with Alameda Parkway	2.3	6,169	N39.40633	W105.11515
C	Trail jct. on Red Rocks access	3.1	6,024	N39.40218	W105.11765
D	Jct. with Morrison Slide Trail	4.1	6,525	N39.40556	W105.12457

The Route Description

From the parking lot, cross Route 26, turn left (north) alongside the road, and look for an obvious wide and moderately rocky trail ascending the ridge to the east. Run up the steep pitch past a closed gate at mile 0.4 (6540), and turn right just before a second closed gate. This takes you just west of the Dakota Ridge crest. You will pass signs on the left warning of a shooting range. You will gradually leave behind the noise of I-70 as you top the crest and enter a lightly wooded area. The trail is intermittently rocky as it shifts slightly to the east side of the ridge and descends to a crossing with Alameda Parkway at mile 2.3 (6170). Cross Alameda Parkway and turn right on the other side of the road, staying to the left (east) of a set of concrete barriers. After a few hundred yards, the trail continues straight ahead while Alameda Parkway turns away to the right.

The trail shifts up to the Dakota Ridge crest and drops down the other side to Hogback Road. Cross Hogback Road and turn right. After a few yards, turn left (west) onto the Red Rocks access road and cross a small bridge. About 200 yards from the road entrance at mile 3.1 (6020), turn left onto an unmarked trail. It switchbacks uphill, crossing a dirt road and then a paved road. After crossing the paved road, turn right and stay on the Red Rocks Trail for the duration of the run. The trail ascends steeply along the west side of beautiful rock formations to a junction with the Morrison Slide Trail at mile 4.1 (6530).

Stay on the Red Rocks Trail, topping out shortly thereafter. From here, the remainder of the trail winds gradually downhill, though there are numerous dips into stream beds involving sharp turns in the trail. The Morrison Slide Trail appears at the end of this segment, merging in from the left just prior to a stream crossing. Stay on the Red Rocks Trail through open fields. Be sure to stay on the trail as it takes a hard right turn just before the parking lot; otherwise you'll end up in someone's back yard! Pass the park bathrooms on the left and drop into the parking lot at mile 5.9 (6330).

Reynolds Park Loop 34

On the crest of the Raven's Roost Trail.

The first mile is difficult, due to the steep grade. However, you are rewarded with fine views of the Cathedral Spires to the south and panoramic vistas to the west when you top out on the Eagle's View Trail. This route can also be shortened prior to Foxton Road.

Location: 19.0 miles west of C-470
Distance/Type: 5.3 miles loop
Running Time: 1.25 hours
Starting Elevation: 7,240 feet
Elevation Gain: 1,470 feet
Best Season: March through October
Jurisdiction: Jefferson County Open Space
(Reynolds Park)
Map(s): *Trails Illustrated # 135*
Permits/Fees: None

Grade: The first mile is quite steep, as well as the first half of the Hummingbird Trail, located near the end of the route. The route is well-maintained through the Raven's Roost, Eagle's View, and Hummingbird Trails, but contains a fair number of rocks on the Elkhorn and Songbird Trails. There is some loose gravel on the Hummingbird Trail.

Getting There: From the junction of C-470 and Route 285, travel west on Route 285 for 14.0 miles and take the exit ramp for Foxton Road. Loop under the highway and then south for 5.0 miles on Foxton Road to the trailhead, which is on the right side of the road.

Rating

Moderate

Mileage

0.0 Start out of parking lot.
0.1 Turn northwest on Elkhorn Trail.
0.4 Go west on Raven's Roost Trail.
1.3 Turn south on Eagle's View Trail.
2.0 Head north on Eagle's View Trail.
3.3 Turn east on Oxen Draw Trail.
3.6 Head east on Songbird Trail.
5.3 Arrive back at parking lot.

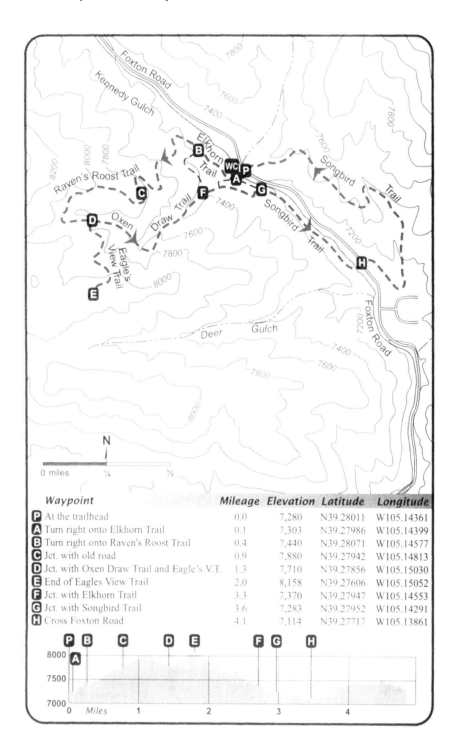

Waypoint	Mileage	Elevation	Latitude	Longitude
P At the trailhead	0.0	7,280	N39.28011	W105.14361
A Turn right onto Elkhorn Trail	0.1	7,303	N39.27986	W105.14399
B Turn right onto Raven's Roost Trail	0.4	7,440	N39.28071	W105.14577
C Jct. with old road	0.9	7,880	N39.27942	W105.14813
D Jct. with Oxen Draw Trail and Eagle's V.T.	1.3	7,710	N39.27856	W105.15030
E End of Eagles View Trail	2.0	8,158	N39.27606	W105.15052
F Jct. with Elkhorn Trail	3.3	7,370	N39.27947	W105.14553
G Jct. with Songbird Trail	3.6	7,283	N39.27952	W105.14291
H Cross Foxton Road	4.1	7,114	N39.27717	W105.13861

The Route Description

Enter the trail system through the gate at the southwest corner of the parking lot, and run slightly uphill and past a bathroom on your right. At mile 0.1 (7300), turn right onto the Elkhorn Trail, which passes above and to the right of the bathroom. The trail climbs immediately. There are some steep sections here, with an average angle of ascent of eleven degrees for the first mile. At a fork in the trail at mile 0.4 (7440), turn right onto the Raven's Roost Trail. Though the trail is wide and smooth, there are several steep sections that will leave you winded. Ignore an old road that splits off to the right at mile 0.9 (7880) and continue on the Raven's Roost Trail.

At a fork in the trail at mile 1.3 (8160) that splits between the Oxen Draw and Eagle's View Trails, turn right onto the Eagle's View Trail. This fine trail will take you uphill through pine forests along a series of switchbacks that open up onto a wide ridgeline that yields excellent views of the Cathedral Spires to the south. The trail ends at a private property marker at mile 2.0 (7370). Turn around and run back to the trail junction with the Oxen Draw Trail at mile 2.7 (8160). This time, turn right onto the Oxen Draw Trail. The route becomes somewhat rockier here as the path rolls southeast through pine forests. At mile 3.3 (7370), turn right at the junction with the Elkhorn Trail. If you wish to terminate the run at this point, turn left and you will be back in the parking lot after another 0.3 miles, with a total mileage of 3.6.

Assuming you continue for the longer run, ignore a left turn onto the Oxen Draw Trail shortly thereafter and continue to a trail junction at mile 3.6 (7280), where you turn right onto the Songbird Trail. You are now heading south through a mix of meadow and trees, with Foxton Road visible through the trees to your left. The trail crosses Foxton Road at mile 4.1 (7110) and ascends steeply up the hillside on the other side of the valley. Ignore the Chickadee Trail on the right and toil up the hillside. You will gain about 500 vertical feet in less than a mile. Top out on an open ridge with clear views to the south and west. Trot down the gravelly path to Foxton Road. Look both ways on Foxton Road before crossing, and enter the parking lot at mile 5.3 (7280).

35 Shadow Mountain Loop

A very popular trail for local dog owners, so be careful as you make your way across the loop. Additionally, some road construction may alter the directions for this route at the intersection of 285 and 73. Be sure to check current driving directions.

Kiosk at the trailhead

Rating

Easy

Classics

Mileage

GO

0.0 Start north on Junction House Trail.
0.6 Bear north on Shadow Pine Loop.
1.4 Continue northwest on Shadow Pine Loop.
3.4 Turn south on Junction House Trail.
4.0 Arrive back at parking lot.

Location: 15.0 miles west of C-470, a short distance north of Route 285
Distance/Type: 4.0 miles loop
Running Time: 45 minutes
Starting Elevation: 8,020 feet
Elevation Gain: 280 feet
Best Season: April through October
Jurisdiction: Jefferson County Open Space (Flying J Ranch Park), Denver Mtn. Parks
Map(s): *Trails Illustrated # 100*
Permits/Fees: None

Grade: Easy, with a two degree average angle of ascent. The trail winds amongst pine forests for most of its length, punctuated by occasional glades. The trail is smooth, with minimal rocks and roots.

Getting There: From the intersection of C-470 and Route 285, drive west on Route 285 for 13.7 miles to the right turnoff onto Route 73 at Conifer. There will be a traffic light immediately after the turnoff. Turn right, go north on Route 73 for 1.2 miles, turn left onto Shadow Mountain Drive, and immediately turn right into the trailhead parking lot.

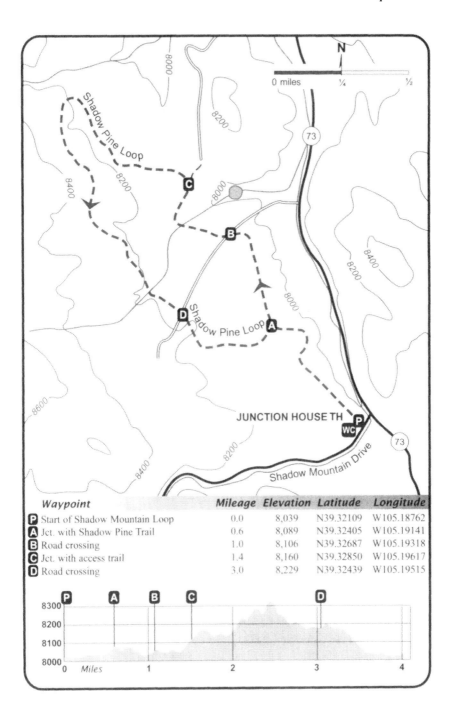

Waypoint	Mileage	Elevation	Latitude	Longitude
P Start of Shadow Mountain Loop	0.0	8,039	N39.32109	W105.18762
A Jct. with Shadow Pine Trail	0.6	8,089	N39.32405	W105.19141
B Road crossing	1.0	8,106	N39.32687	W105.19318
C Jct. with access trail	1.4	8,160	N39.32850	W105.19617
D Road crossing	3.0	8,229	N39.32439	W105.19515

Pounding along the Shadow Mountain Loop.

The Route Description

Begin on the Junction House Trail, which travels alongside Route 73 for a short distance and then turns away from the road and crosses a pleasant wooden bridge near a set of power lines. At mile 0.6 (8090), turn right onto Shadow Pine Trail and continue through open pine forest until you reach a dirt road. At mile 1.0 (8110), cross the road and continue straight along a double track gravel path that gradually narrows and becomes less clear. You will be able to see the Schoonhoven Pond some distance off to the right.   Avoid a right turn at mile 1.4 (8160) onto an access trail to a local housing development. The trail temporarily becomes fainter in this area. Continue around a loop that takes you through dense pine forest and past the trail's high point of 8,280 feet. At mile 3.0 (8,230), cross a later section of the same dirt road that you crossed earlier. There will be a private property sign a short ways up the road to your right. The trail continues on the other side of the road through more pine forest and glades to the junction with the Junction House Trail. Continue back down the gentle Junction House Trail to the trailhead at mile 4.0 (8040).

South Valley Park Medley 36

Red rock formation along the
Coyote Song Trail.

This route is almost entirely devoid of tree cover, so run it on a cool day or early in the morning. The first loop has superb views of unusual red rock formations that sprout up throughout the park. The second loop is dominated by the silver Lockheed headquarters building to the west. Be sure to wave at the security guard shack as you run by.

Rating

Easy

Location: 3.5 miles southwest of C-470
Distance/Type: 6.2 miles medley
Running Time: 1.25 hours
Starting Elevation: 5,470 feet
Elevation Gain: 760 feet
Best Season: March into November
Jurisdiction: Jefferson County Open Space (South Valley Park)
Map(s): *Trails Illustrated # 100*
Permits/Fees: None

Grade: Beginner, with a barely discernible angle of ascent after the first half-mile. The trail is extremely well-maintained through the first loop, and then converts to smooth single track for the second loop.

Getting There: From the junction of C-470 and Wadsworth, travel south on Wadsworth for 0.4 miles and turn right (west) onto Deer Creek Canyon Road. Continue on this road for two miles, turning left at a road junction. Continue for 1.1 miles, and then turn right into a parking lot for the clearly marked South Valley Park.

Mileage *GO*

0.0 Start north on Coyote Song Trail.
1.3 Go South on Swallow Trail.
2.2 Head southwest on Swallow Trail.
2.9 Head either north or south on Grazing Elk Trail.
5.0 Rejoin beginning of Grazing Elk Trail. Head east.
5.6 Turn southeast on connector trail.
5.8 Go south on Coyote Song Trail.
6.2 Arrive back at parking lot.

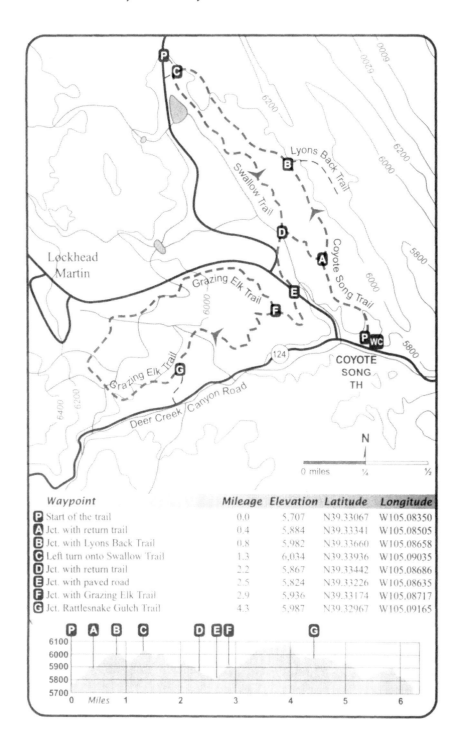

Waypoint		Mileage	Elevation	Latitude	Longitude
P	Start of the trail	0.0	5,707	N39.33067	W105.08350
A	Jct. with return trail	0.4	5,884	N39.33341	W105.08505
B	Jct. with Lyons Back Trail	0.8	5,982	N39.33660	W105.08658
C	Left turn onto Swallow Trail	1.3	6,034	N39.33936	W105.09035
D	Jct. with return trail	2.2	5,867	N39.33442	W105.08686
E	Jct. with paved road	2.5	5,824	N39.33226	W105.08635
F	Jct. with Grazing Elk Trail	2.9	5,936	N39.33174	W105.08717
G	Jct. Rattlesnake Gulch Trail	4.3	5,987	N39.32967	W105.09165

The Route Description

From the parking lot, run up the wide and well-graded Coyote Song Trail to the north. A junction will come in from the left at 0.4 miles (5880); ignore this and continue straight, with beautiful views of rock formations on all sides. At mile 0.8 (5980), the Lyons Back Trail branches off to the right. Continue straight ahead, going gradually uphill. At the top of the hill at mile 1.3 (6030), turn left onto the Swallow Trail. The Swallow Trail passes next to several picnic tables and a parking area before looping back to the south. There is a small restricted-access pond on the right. Stay south-bound on this hikers-only trail.

The trail forks at mile 2.2 (5870). If you go left, the route will take you back to your car, with a total mileage of 2.8. If you take the right turn, the trail goes downhill and meets a private access road that leads onto Lockheed property. After crossing the private road at mile 2.5 (5820), the trail angles up through the only tree cover on the route, quickly emerging onto a broad grassy plateau. At mile 2.9 (5940), the trail meets the Grazing Elk Trail, which runs in a loop around this plateau. You may take the loop in either direction. The highest point on the run (6,080 feet) is at the far western end of the loop, nearest the Lockheed headquarters building. After looping past the Lockheed building and turning back east, you will pass the Rattlesnake Gulch Trail at mile 4.3 (5990). After completing the loop around the Grazing Elk Trail at mile 5.0 (5940), run back down through the short stretch of trees to the private road. You may turn right onto the road and be back in the parking lot in a few minutes. However, to avoid the pavement, re-cross the road and run back uphill for 0.3 miles to the junction with a connector trail at mile 5.6 (5870) that takes you from the Swallow Trail back to the Coyote Song Trail. The connector trail is a quick 0.2 miles. At its termination with the Coyote Song Trail, turn right and jog back down to the end of the run at mile 6.2 (5710) in the parking lot.

37 Carpenter Peak Trail

An excellent trail for a hard morning run. However, there are a few sharp switchbacks with steps that will probably require you to come to a complete stop to make the turn. Also, this low and east-facing park can be quite hot in the summer, so either run early or during a different season. When returning to your car, look for rattlesnakes that like to rest in the warmth of the asphalt parking area.

Looking east from the middle of the Carpenter Peak Trail.

Rating

Moderate

Mileage *GO*

0.0 Start west out of parking lot.
0.1 Go south on Willow Creek Trail.
0.3 Bear south and then west on Carpenter Peak Trail.
3.1 Continue north on Carpenter Peak Trail.
3.2 Turnaround on Carpenter Peak Trail and re-trace route.
6.4 Arrive back at parking lot.

Location: 15.0 miles south of C-470, inside Roxborough State Park
Distance/Type: 6.4 miles trail
Running Time: 1.5 hours
Starting Elevation: 6,160 feet
Elevation Gain: 1,070 feet
Best Season: March through November
Jurisdiction: Roxborough State Park, Pike National Forest
Map(s): *Trails Illustrated # 135*
Permits/Fees: $5 daily park fee required

Grade: Moderate, with a 5 degree average angle of ascent. The trail is well-maintained, with few rocks.

Getting There: From the junction of C-470 and Santa Fe, travel south on Santa Fe for 4.0 miles and turn right (west) onto Titan Road. Continue on Titan for 3.0 miles, following it around a ninety-degree bend to the left (south), where its name changes to the Rampart Range Road. Follow this road for 6.5 miles

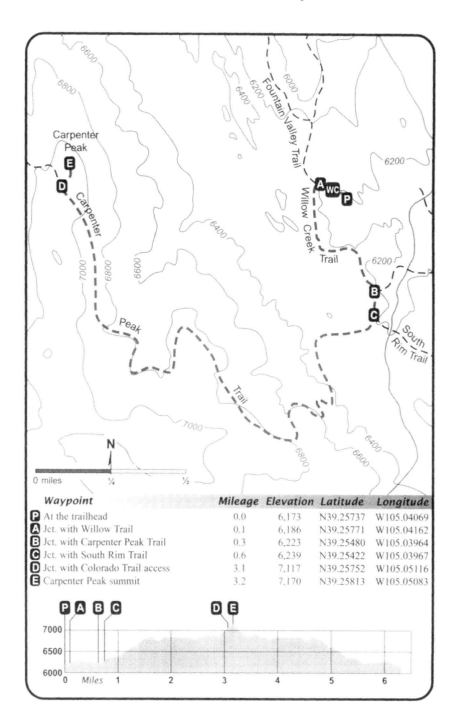

Waypoint	Mileage	Elevation	Latitude	Longitude
P At the trailhead	0.0	6,173	N39.25737	W105.04069
A Jct. with Willow Trail	0.1	6,186	N39.25771	W105.04162
B Jct. with Carpenter Peak Trail	0.3	6,223	N39.25480	W105.03964
C Jct. with South Rim Trail	0.6	6,239	N39.25422	W105.03967
D Jct. with Colorado Trail access	3.1	7,117	N39.25752	W105.05116
E Carpenter Peak summit	3.2	7,170	N39.25813	W105.05083

Roxborough Park is famous for flower strewn meadows and red rock formations.

to a left turn into the Roxborough State Park. Pay the entrance fee at the ranger station and continue to the end of the road for another 2.2 miles, park in the lot on the right.

The Route Description

From the parking lot, follow the access road around a corner to the visitor center. Take the Willow Trail at mile 0.1 (6190), whose entrance is directly across an access road from the visitor center. Immediately enter close foliage, occasionally breaking out for views of spectacular up thrusting rock formations in all directions. The trail will soon split at mile 0.3 (6220), with the Willow Trail going left. Take the right turn, following signs to Carpenter Peak and the Colorado Trail. Bypass a turnoff to the South Rim Trail at mile 0.6 (6240) and continue up the Carpenter Peak Trail, which soon crosses a dirt road.

Cross the road and follow the trail uphill at a steady angle for the next 2.6 miles. The trail gradually curls around to the northwest, angling gently upward. At mile 3.1 (7120), a side trail branches off to the left (west), heading for the Colorado Trail. Turn right to continue to the summit of Carpenter Peak. Trail maintenance degrades rapidly near the summit, so it is advisable to walk the final few yards. Cool off on the summit at mile 3.2 (7170) for a few moments, and then turn around and head back down the trail. You will reach the parking lot at mile 6.4 (7160).

Plymouth Mountain Trail 38

Running along the Meadowlark Trail.

In the summer, try to run this trail early on the weekends, so that you can see hot air balloons rising about Chatfield Reservoir directly to the east. Also, the beginning and end of the route are east facing, so run early or late in order to avoid the heat.

Rating

Moderate

Location: 4.7 miles southwest of C-470
Distance/Type: 5.7 miles trail
Running Time: 1.25 hours
Starting Elevation: 6,070 feet
Elevation Gain: 1,820 feet
Best Season: March through November
Jurisdiction: Jefferson County Open Space (Deer Creek Canyon Park)
Map(s): Trails Illustrated # 100
Permits/Fees: None

Grade: Moderately steep, with an eight degree average angle of ascent. The trail is well-maintained in the hiker-only segment, requires a walk in a short steep section, and contains some embedded rocks and rocky steps in the loop part of the trail.

Getting There: From the junction of C-470 and Wadsworth, travel south on Wadsworth for 0.4 miles and turn right (west) onto Deer Creek Canyon Road. Continue on this road for two miles, turning left at a road junction. Continue for 1.8 miles, and then turn left into a subdivision entrance that borders on Deer Creek Canyon Park. Follow the signs to the parking lot for this park, which is 4.3 miles from C-470. The trail begins just beyond and to the right of the bathrooms.

GO

Mileage

0.0 Start west on Meadowlark Trail.
1.6 Head west on Plymouth Creek Trail.
2.1 Go south on Plymouth Mountain Trail.
2.4 Continue West on Plymouth Mountain Trail.
3.7 Turn north on Plymouth Creek Trail.
4.1 Head east on Meadowlark Trail.

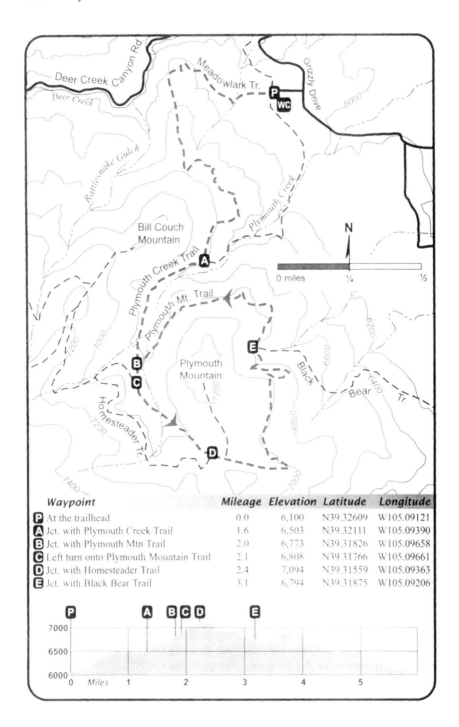

Waypoint	Mileage	Elevation	Latitude	Longitude
P At the trailhead	0.0	6,100	N39.32609	W105.09121
A Jct. with Plymouth Creek Trail	1.6	6,503	N39.32111	W105.09390
B Jct. with Plymouth Mtn Trail	2.0	6,773	N39.31826	W105.09658
C Left turn onto Plymouth Mountain Trail	2.1	6,808	N39.31766	W105.09661
D Jct. with Homesteader Trail	2.4	7,094	N39.31559	W105.09363
E Jct. with Black Bear Trail	3.1	6,794	N39.31875	W105.09206

The Route Description

From the bathrooms at the parking lot, take the Meadowlark Trail, which rapidly shrinks from a wide double track to a well-graded single track that slabs up the east side of Bill Couch Mountain. You are in full view of the parking lot for the first half-mile, so show good form! The trail turns south and descends slightly to cross a small bridge and join with the Plymouth Creek Trail at mile 1.6 (6500). Turn right onto the Plymouth Creek Trail. This trail is shared with mountain bikers, and shows much more usage. The trail soon becomes steeper for a brutal fifty-yard stretch, for which you should probably slow to a walk. This is a rock-strewn area, and can be treacherous.

Pass the Plymouth Mountain Trail on your left at mile 2.0 (6780). You will be coming back down it in a half-hour, but for now let it pass, continuing up the Plymouth Creek Trail. There continues to be steep sections, though the running surface is smoother here. Take the Plymouth Mountain Trail at mile 2.1 (6810), ignoring the Plymouth Creek Trail, which turns right here. You will reach a three-way "T" junction at mile 2.4 (7090) with the Homesteader Trail. Turn left here to stay on the Plymouth Mountain Trail. The elevation reaches its maximum at the beginning of this section, and then drops almost 300 feet over the next two miles, with most of it occurring in the first mile. You can ignore the Black Bear Trail which departs down and to the right at mile 3.1 (6790). There are two uphill sections in the remainder of this loop, with the harder one appearing just before the trail loops back down to its junction with the Plymouth Creek Trail. Also, watch out for embedded rocks and small rocky ledges in this area.

Turn right onto the Plymouth Creek Trail at mile 3.7 (6780). Though the angle of descent may encourage you to fly down this section, slow down and be aware of loose rocks, especially in the 50-yard area noted earlier. This is especially dangerous when the rocks are wet or loosely covered with sand. Turn left at mile 4.1 (6500) and cross a small bridge to access the Meadowlark Trail. There is an initial uphill jog to the north, followed by easy cruising turns through the switchbacks and down to the parking lot at mile 5.7 (6100).

39 Red Mesa Loop

The beginning portion of this run is the same one used for the Plymouth Mountain Trail, with the key difference being the superb Red Mountain Loop at the highest elevation of the course. Try Golden Eagle and Homesteader Trails which are hiker only.

The well-graded Meadowlark Trail climbs up the side of Bill Couch Mountain.

Rating

Moderate

GO

Mileage

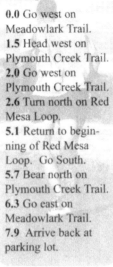

0.0 Go west on Meadowlark Trail.
1.5 Head west on Plymouth Creek Trail.
2.0 Go west on Plymouth Creek Trail.
2.6 Turn north on Red Mesa Loop.
5.1 Return to beginning of Red Mesa Loop. Go South.
5.7 Bear north on Plymouth Creek Trail.
6.3 Go east on Meadowlark Trail.
7.9 Arrive back at parking lot.

Location: 4.7 miles southwest of C-470
Distance/Type: 7.9 miles loop
Running Time: 1.5 hours
Starting Elevation: 6,070 feet
Elevation Gain: 2,080 feet
Best Season: March through November
Jurisdiction: Jefferson County Open Space (Deer Creek Canyon Parks)
Map(s): *Trails Illustrated # 100*
Permits/Fees: None

Grade: Moderately steep, with a six degree average angle of ascent. The trail is well-maintained in the hiker-only segment, requires a walk in a short steep section, and contains some sandy sections and exposed water bars in the loop part of the trail.

Getting There: From the junction of C-470 and Wadsworth, travel south on Wadsworth for 0.4 miles and turn right (west) onto Deer Creek Canyon Road. Continue on this road for two miles, turning left at a road junction. Continue for 1.8 miles, and then turn left into a subdivision entrance that borders on Deer Creek Canyon Park. Follow the signs to the parking lot for this park, which is 4.3 miles from C-470. The trail begins just beyond and to the right of the bathrooms.

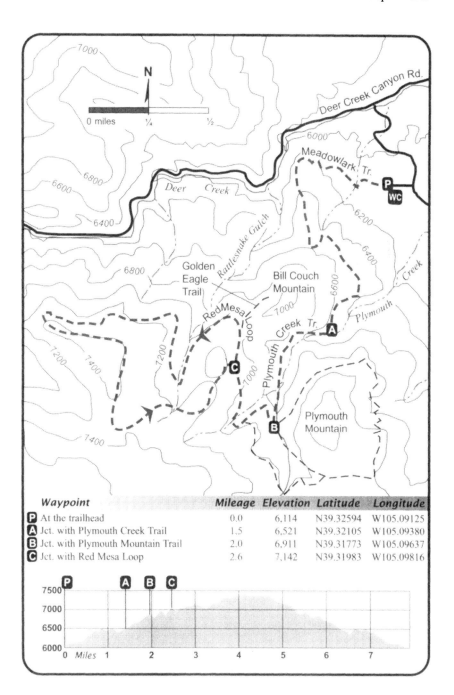

Waypoint	Mileage	Elevation	Latitude	Longitude
P At the trailhead	0.0	6,114	N39.32594	W105.09125
A Jct. with Plymouth Creek Trail	1.5	6,521	N39.32105	W105.09380
B Jct. with Plymouth Mountain Trail	2.0	6,911	N39.31773	W105.09637
C Jct. with Red Mesa Loop	2.6	7,142	N39.31983	W105.09816

The Route Description

From the bathrooms at the parking lot, take the Meadowlark Trail, which rapidly shrinks from a wide double track to a well-graded single track that slabs up the east side of Bill Couch Mountain. You are in full view of the parking lot for the first half-mile, so show good form! The trail turns south and descends slightly to cross a small bridge and joins with the Plymouth Creek Trail at mile 1.5 (6520). Turn right onto the Plymouth Creek Trail. This trail is shared with mountain bikers, and shows much more usage. The trail soon becomes more steep for a brutal fifty-yard stretch, for which you should probably slow to a walk. This is a rock-strewn area, and can be treacherous.

You will reach a three-way "T" junction at mile 2.0 (6910), where the Plymouth Mountain Trail goes left. Turn right to stay on the Plymouth Creek Trail. Continue for another 0.6 miles through occasional water bars and short sandy sections to a junction with the Red Mesa Loop at mile 2.6 (7140). This is a three-way junction. By turning right onto the Red Mesa Loop, you can run gradually uphill for the next mile, passing an optional out-and-back run on the Golden Eagle Trail that takes you to a viewing point and back; this option will add one mile to the route. The loop passes through fine open pine forests on generally firm single track, returning you to the three-way junction. The high point of the route, at 7,420 feet, is just over half-way through the loop.

Return to the beginning of the loop at mile 5.1 (7140) and turn right to descend back to the junction with the Plymouth Mountain Trail, which you will encounter at mile 5.7 (6910). Turn left onto the Plymouth Creek Trail. Though the angle of descent may encourage you to fly down this, turn on the brakes and be aware of loose rocks, especially in the 50-yard area noted earlier. This is especially dangerous when the rocks are wet or loosely covered with sand. Turn left at mile 6.3 (6520) and cross a small bridge to access the Meadowlark Trail. There is an initial uphill jog to the north, followed by easy cruising turns through the switchbacks and down to the parking lot. The parking lot will appear at mile 7.9 (6110).

Roxborough Park Medley 40

*T*his beautiful park has some amazing red-rock formations, which also happen to make it extremely popular for hikers. Due to its enclosure by dense shrubbery in numerous areas, you will not see them coming. Additionally, this low and east-facing park can be quite hot in the summer, so run early. Finally, avoid the South Rim Trail for at least a day after any significant rainfall, since the clay base of the trail becomes astonishingly sloppy when wet.

Along the Fountain Valley Trail.

Location: 15.0 miles south of C-470, inside Roxborough State Park
Distance/Type: 5.1 miles medley
Running Time: 1.0 hour
Starting Elevation: 6,150 feet
Elevation Gain: 690 feet
Best Season: Nearly year-round
Jurisdiction: Roxborough State Park
Map(s): *Trails Illustrated # 135*
Permits/Fees: $5 daily park fee required

Rating
Easy

Classics

Grade: Easy, with a two degree average angle of ascent. The trail is wide and perfectly groomed during the first loop on the Fountain Valley Trail, turning into narrow single track on the Willow and South Rim Trails.

Getting There: From the junction of C-470 and Santa Fe, travel south on Santa Fe for 4.0 miles and turn right (west) onto Titan Road. Continue on Titan for 3.0 miles, following it around a ninety-degree

Mileage
0.0 Start north on Fountain Valley Trail.
0.3 Bear northeast on Fountain Valley Trail.
2.3 Head south on Willow Creek Trail.
2.8 Go south on the South Rim Trail.
4.7 Turn west on the park access road.
5.1 Arrive back at the parking lot.

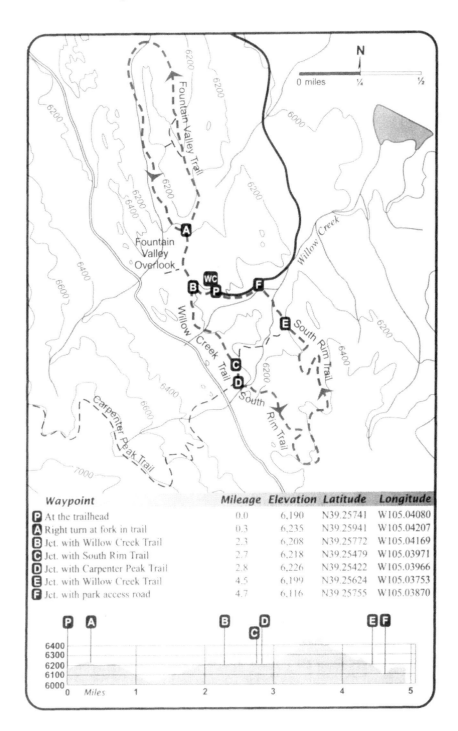

Waypoint	Mileage	Elevation	Latitude	Longitude
P At the trailhead	0.0	6,190	N39.25741	W105.04080
A Right turn at fork in trail	0.3	6,235	N39.25941	W105.04207
B Jct. with Willow Creek Trail	2.3	6,208	N39.25772	W105.04169
C Jct. with South Rim Trail	2.7	6,218	N39.25479	W105.03971
D Jct. with Carpenter Peak Trail	2.8	6,226	N39.25422	W105.03966
E Jct. with Willow Creek Trail	4.5	6,199	N39.25624	W105.03753
F Jct. with park access road	4.7	6,116	N39.25755	W105.03870

bend to the left (south), where its name changes to the Rampart Range Road. Follow this road for 6.5 miles to a left turn into the Roxborough State Park. Pay the entrance fee at the ranger station and continue to the end of the road in 2.2 miles, parking in the lot on the right. The trail begins beyond the parking lot, behind the visitor center.

The Route Description

Starting behind the visitor center, take the Fountain Valley Trail north on an easy loop around the park perimeter. Take the right turn at the fork located at mile 0.3 (6240). There are dozens of red rock up thrusts in this area, making for a stunning run. The trail gradually goes downhill along a broad and manicured path, turning around for a loop back at a ruined cabin. Run back to the visitor center via the backside of the Fountain Valley Trail, passing close to massive red rock formations. During dusk, you will have a good chance of seeing deer in this area.

Directly across from the visitor center, at mile 2.3 (6210), is the beginning of the Willow Creek Trail. Plunge into a sea of low scrub trees, passing through occasional glades. Stay to the right at mile 2.7 (6220), so that you can shift to the South Rim Trail. You will come to a three-way junction at mile 2.8 (6230) with the Carpenter Peak Trail and South Rim Trail. See the Carpenter Peak Trail route description for a review of this excellent run. For this route, however, turn left onto the South Rim Trail.

The trail winds up and down, gradually ascending to a high point of 6,400 feet, where you can rest on a park bench. Then run back down through a series of switchbacks to a junction with the Willow Trail at mile 4.5 (6200). Continue straight ahead from this junction (do not take a hard left), which brings you to the park access road at mile 4.7 (6120). The trail becomes quite narrow just before the road and travels left and parallel to the road before crossing over and continuing on the north side of the road. The trail passes to the right of a small parking area and finishes back in the main parking lot at mile 5.1 (6120).

41 Bluffs Park Loop

*T*his trail would normally be too short to be worthy of attention, but it is very close to a large number of people who work in the Denver Tech Center area or who live in the Highlands Ranch area, and so makes a good lunch-time or after-work run. There is exactly one tree on this route, so do not rely on shade; also, due to the exposure, this is not a good run on stormy days when the risk of lightning is high. There are a number of signs posted warning of rattlesnakes in the area. This is the Tinsley Trail, but the name is rarely marked on the route.

A view of Highlands Ranch on the north side of the loop.

Rating

Easy

Mileage

GO

0.0 Start south out of parking lot. Then head west.
0.6 Continue southwest on access trail.
1.2 Bear south on access trail.
1.4 Head east on access trail.
2.2 Continue west and then north on access trail.
2.7 Arrive back at parking lot.

Location: 2.0 miles south of C-470 and slightly west of I-25
Distance/Type: 2.7 miles loop
Running Time: 30 minutes
Starting Elevation: 6,040 feet
Elevation Gain: 380 feet
Best Season: Nearly year-round
Jurisdiction: Douglas County
Map(s): USGS 7 ½' - Highlands Ranch
Permits/Fees: none

Grade: Easy, with a 3 degree average angle of ascent. The trail is very well-maintained double track, with no rocks.

Getting There: From the intersection of C-470 and Yosemite, turn south onto Yosemite and travel 1.5 miles to the intersection with Lincoln Avenue. Continue south on Yosemite for another half-mile until you reach a turnoff on the right into a spacious parking lot for the Bluffs Regional Park.

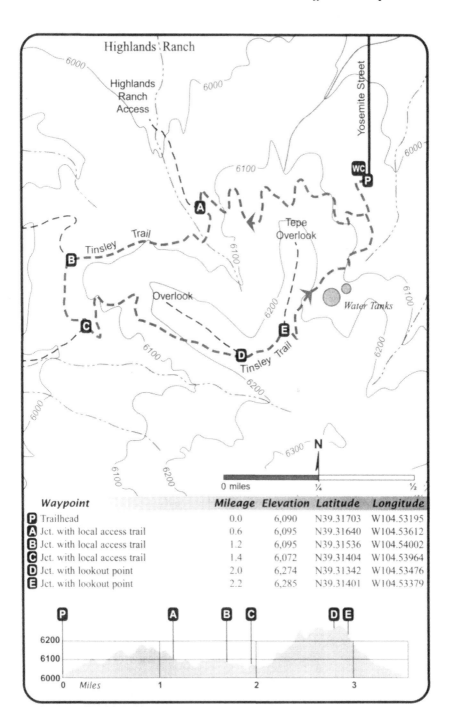

Waypoint		Mileage	Elevation	Latitude	Longitude
P	Trailhead	0.0	6,090	N39.31703	W104.53195
A	Jct. with local access trail	0.6	6,095	N39.31640	W104.53612
B	Jct. with local access trail	1.2	6,095	N39.31536	W104.54002
C	Jct. with local access trail	1.4	6,072	N39.31404	W104.53964
D	Jct. with lookout point	2.0	6,274	N39.31342	W104.53476
E	Jct. with lookout point	2.2	6,285	N39.31401	W104.53379

The Route Description

From the parking lot, start at the obvious trailhead between the picnic table and bathroom and immediately turn left (south). After 100 yards, turn right at the rattlesnake warning sign and ascend through several switchbacks on wide double track to a low ridge with views to the north and east. The enormous housing development to the northwest is Highlands Ranch. Travel along the side of the ridge for two tenths of a mile, and then drop down to a junction at mile 0.6 (6100) with a small trail that splits off to the right; this gives park access to Highlands Ranch residents. Continue to the left.

The trail dips slightly as it curls around to the west and then south along the sides of the small mesa that forms the center of the park, reaching another turnoff at mile 1.2 (6100) on the right that gives access to local residents, as well as a similar junction at mile 1.4 (6070). Continue to the left. There is yet another turnoff to the local neighborhood (this one turning to the right) at mile 1.8 (6070). Stay left here as the trail turns sharply back on itself to the north and then traverses across the west face of the mesa as it climbs past a stone wall on the left and passes the only tree in the park on the left. It reaches a high point of 6,290 feet, where views are outstanding in all directions. You may take a short side trip to the left at this point to a lookout point - if so; add two tenths of a mile to your total mileage. Otherwise, continue straight ahead.

Continue across the top of the mesa to another turnoff at mile 2.2 (6290) on the left that reaches a park bench and memorial to the county planning director. If you take this option, add four tenths of a mile to your total mileage. Otherwise, continue straight ahead. The trail plunges down through several switchbacks toward several county water tanks. Pass them on the left, ignoring a side road on the right that leads to them. Arrive in the parking lot at mile 2.7 (6090), ready for another loop.

Castlewood Canyon Loop 42

The ruins of Castlewood Dam.

The trail drops quickly into Castlewood Canyon and stays there until reaching the ruins of the old Castlewood Canyon Dam, which is over 100 years old. The canyon portion of this run affords one an easy cruise through the spectacular canyon walls. Something important to note is that the Rim Rock Trail can be difficult to follow in places, and also requires a stiff hike of several hundred vertical feet to reach. Rattlesnakes have been found on the Rim Rock Trail.

Rating

Moderate

Location: 9.0 miles southeast of Castle Rock
Distance/Type: 6.7 miles loop
Running Time: 1.25 hours
Starting Elevation: 6,280 feet
Elevation Gain: 800 feet
Best Season: March to November
Jurisdiction: Castlewood Canyon State Park
Map(s): *USGS 7 ½'* - Russellville Gulch
Permits/Fees: $5 daily park fee required

Grade: Easy to moderate. The difficulty here is not elevation gain (with the exception of the Rim Rock Trail), but rather the constant rock ledges, steps, and frequent trail windings that must be negotiated.

Getting There: From I-25, take Exit # 182 in Castle Rock, pass over the highway going eastbound, and turn right onto Route 86. Follow this road east for 6.7 miles until you reach Castlewood Canyon Road. Turn right (south) onto this road and drive 2.1 miles to the park entrance. Pay the admission fee and con-

Mileage *GO*

0.0 Start west on the Homestead Trail.
0.4 Head south on Creek Bottom Trail.
2.1 Bear west on Inner Canyon Trail.
2.4 Go south on Lake Gulch Trail.
3.2 Head northeast through parking area onto nature trail.
6.3 Go north on Homestead Trail.
6.7 Arrive back at parking lot.

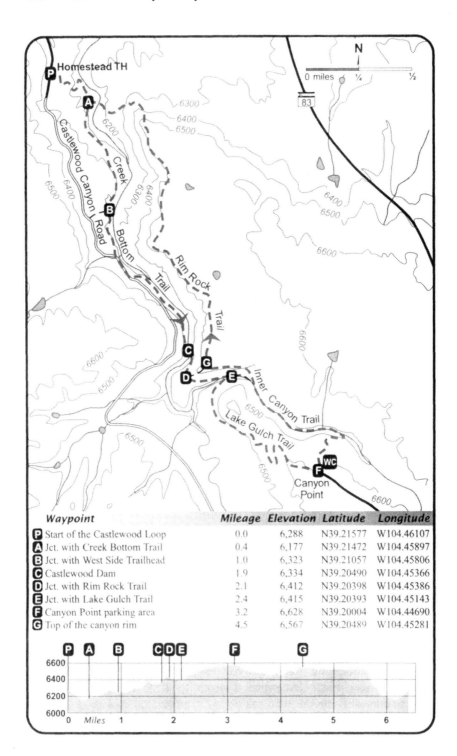

Waypoint	Mileage	Elevation	Latitude	Longitude
P Start of the Castlewood Loop	0.0	6,288	N39.21577	W104.46107
A Jct. with Creek Bottom Trail	0.4	6,177	N39.21472	W104.45897
B Jct. with West Side Trailhead	1.0	6,323	N39.21057	W104.45806
C Castlewood Dam	1.9	6,334	N39.20490	W104.45366
D Jct. with Rim Rock Trail	2.1	6,412	N39.20398	W104.45386
E Jct. with Lake Gulch Trail	2.4	6,415	N39.20393	W104.45143
F Canyon Point parking area	3.2	6,628	N39.20004	W104.44690
G Top of the canyon rim	4.5	6,567	N39.20489	W104.45281

tinue for 0.1 miles to the Homestead Trail parking area. If the road turns to dirt, you have gone too far.

The Route Description

The Homestead Trail begins at the northeast corner of the parking lot. Follow this past a trail information sign and down into the canyon. The gradient is moderate, but watch out for rocky steps and sudden turns in the trail. At mile 0.4 (6180), turn right onto the Creek Bottom Trail. This trail winds amongst low trees and shrubbery along the right (south) side of the canyon, affording good views of the cliffs on the opposite side. At mile 1.0 (6320), there is a junction with the West Side Trailhead; turn left to stay on the Creek Bottom Trail. Continue to be careful when running across ledges, stairs, and a large boulder that bridges the trail. The old Castlewood Dam is located at mile 1.9 (6330), which blocks the right side of the canyon. You can take a short side trail to inspect the ruins, or continue past them and turn left to cross a small footbridge that takes you to the other side of the canyon. You are now on the Lake Gulch Trail. If you want to shorten the run, turn left onto the Rim Rock Trail to loop back to the car. Otherwise, continue to follow the Lake Gulch Trail as it turns east.

There is a junction at mile 2.1 (6410) with the Inner Canyon Trail and the Rim Rock Trail; stay right to continue on the Inner Canyon Trail. Continue to mile 2.4 (6420), where there is a junction with the Inner Canyon Trail and the Lake Gulch Trail. Turn right onto the Lake Gulch Trail and follow it around the southern boundary of the park, with views of grazing areas and local homes to the south. The trail terminates at the large Canyon Point parking area at mile 3.2 (6630). Run halfway through the parking lot and turn left onto a short paved nature trail. The Inner Canyon Trail branches away to the left of this trail after 100 yards. Follow the Inner Canyon Trail past a series of interesting bouldering problems, mostly to the right (north) side of the trail. The footing can be tricky here, so watch your step.

The trail merges into the Rim Rock Trail near the old dam that you passed on the way in. The Rim Rock contours along the northeast side of the canyon rim, but to get there you have to climb up several hundred vertical feet of steep rock steps. Good luck running this part! The top of the rim is at mile 4.5 (6570). Once on top, the trail can be hard to follow because it is infrequently marked with small cairns. In general, the trail tends to stay about twenty yards away from the cliff edge. It then drops down and around the north end of the canyon. At mile 6.3 (6180), turn back onto the Homestead Trail and follow it back to the parking lot at mile 6.7 (6290).

43 High Line Canal

*D*espite its considerable length, I have rated this trail as "beginner," due its non-existent elevation changes, easy running surface, and the ability to turn around at any point to return to your car. Though located in south Denver suburbia rather than the mountains, this is such a pleasant route, with its perfectly graded path, overhanging hardwood trees, and expensive nearby homes (at the north end of the trail) that it was eminently deserving of inclusion. But be aware that there are six crossings of South Broadway, a very busy four-lane road. Please proceed carefully at these crossings.

Winter running along the High Line Canal. (Gretchen Hanisch)

Rating

Easy

Mileage

0.0 Start from parking lot.
2.1 Stay left to remain on High Line.
11.2 Go over bridge and then turn left.
14.3 Turn around at Belleview Avenue.
28.6 Arrive back at parking lot.

Location: Littleton and Greenwood Village
Distance/Type: 28.6 miles out and back
Running Time: 5.0 to 6.0 hours
Starting Elevation: 5,530 feet
Elevation Gain: 60 feet
Best Season: Nearly year-round
Jurisdiction: Arapahoe and Douglas Counties
Map(s): USGS 7 ½ ' - Littleton
Permits/Fees: None

Grade: Flat, wide, and perfectly maintained.

Getting There: From the intersection of C-470 and Broadway, go north on Broadway for 0.7 miles and turn left onto West Mineral Avenue. Follow it for 1.1 miles and then turn left onto Peninsula Drive. Immediately turn left into the parking lot.

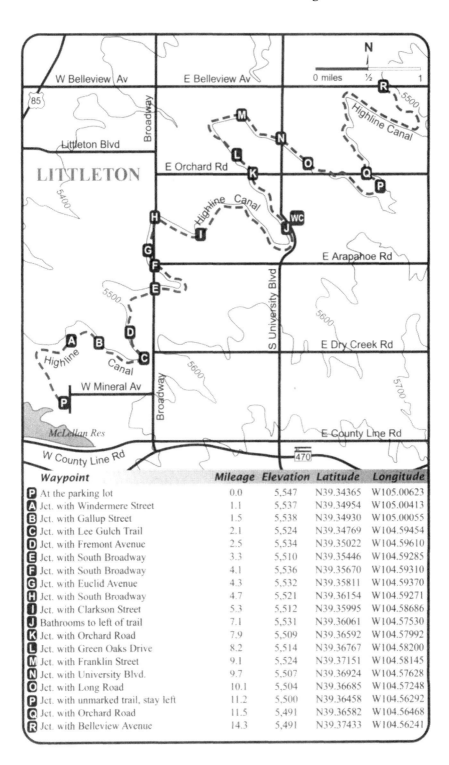

Waypoint	Mileage	Elevation	Latitude	Longitude
P At the parking lot	0.0	5,547	N39.34365	W105.00623
A Jct. with Windermere Street	1.1	5,537	N39.34954	W105.00413
B Jct. with Gallup Street	1.5	5,538	N39.34930	W105.00055
C Jct. with Lee Gulch Trail	2.1	5,524	N39.34769	W104.59454
D Jct. with Fremont Avenue	2.5	5,534	N39.35022	W104.59610
E Jct. with South Broadway	3.3	5,510	N39.35446	W104.59285
F Jct. with South Broadway	4.1	5,536	N39.35670	W104.59310
G Jct. with Euclid Avenue	4.3	5,532	N39.35811	W104.59370
H Jct. with South Broadway	4.7	5,521	N39.36154	W104.59271
I Jct. with Clarkson Street	5.3	5,512	N39.35995	W104.58686
J Bathrooms to left of trail	7.1	5,531	N39.36061	W104.57530
K Jct. with Orchard Road	7.9	5,509	N39.36592	W104.57992
L Jct. with Green Oaks Drive	8.2	5,514	N39.36767	W104.58200
M Jct. with Franklin Street	9.1	5,524	N39.37151	W104.58145
N Jct. with University Blvd.	9.7	5,507	N39.36924	W104.57628
O Jct. with Long Road	10.1	5,504	N39.36685	W104.57248
P Jct. with unmarked trail, stay left	11.2	5,500	N39.36458	W104.56292
Q Jct. with Orchard Road	11.5	5,491	N39.36582	W104.56468
R Jct. with Belleview Avenue	14.3	5,491	N39.37433	W104.56241

The Route Description

The route is the same all the way - wide, perfectly paved, with minimal changes in elevation. There are extraordinarily expensive homes looming over the northern end of the trail, which makes it worthwhile to run all the way to its end. Given the large number of street crossings and minimal elevation changes, this route description is presented as a list of bullet points, with street names, cumulative mile points, and route-finding notes. Please remember that this list of street crossing is one way - you still have to turn around and run the same distance back to your car. The route is as follows:

Street Junction	Mileage
Windermere Street	Mile 1.1
Gallup Street	Mile 1.5
Lee Gulch Trail	Mile 2.1
Fremont Avenue	Mile 2.5
South Broadway	Mile 3.3
South Broadway (2nd)	Mile 4.1
Euclid Avenue	Mile 4.3
South Broadway (3rd)	Mile 4.7
Clarkson Street	Mile 5.3
Bathrooms to left of trail	Mile 7.1
Orchard Road	Mile 7.9
Green Oaks Drive	Mile 8.2
Franklin Street	Mile 9.1
University Blvd.	Mile 9.7
Long Road	Mile 10.1
Unmarked trail	Mile 11.2
Orchard Road	Mile 11.5
Belleview Avenue	Mile 14.3

Colorado Springs Area

In alphabetical order, the trails
itemized in this section are as follows:

Barr Trail
Cap'n Jack's Trail
Lovell Gulch Loop
Mueller State Park Medley
Rampart Reservoir Loop
Stratton Medley
Waldo Canyon Loop

At Rampart Reservoir.

Colorado Springs is dominated by the brooding bulk of Pikes Peak, which looms over the city. The Air Force Academy is located just to the north of town, where the Falcons stadium and Air Force chapel are easily visible from the highway, as well as a number of training aircraft being operated by jittery Academy students. An annual Pikes Peak road race, featuring high octane cars and drivers, winds its way up the Pikes Peak auto road during one weekend each summer, while the considerably slower Pikes Peak Marathon does the same thing without all the octane. The Incline Club specializes in training runners for the marathon. For more information, check their web site at *www.inclineclub.com.*

The main route along which runs are located is Route 24, which begins as a four-lane road, eventually shrinking down to two lanes as it winds west through the mountains. Because the road seems to be used by the entire population of Colorado Springs, try to go out early in the morning for runs, before the road becomes overly congested.

The Air Force Academy used to allow outsiders to run on an excellent loop trail encircling the academy grounds. However, due to terrorist concerns, the trail has been closed to the general public.

For those runners driving down to Colorado Springs from Denver, watch out for the startlingly bad weather on Monument Hill, located just to the north of Colorado Springs on Interstate 25. There can be a fog bank here even on sunny days that rivals the Scottish moors, while conditions in the winter are treacherous enough to make this a good alternative location for the Iditarod sled dog race.

The Colorado Springs region contains two of the finest trail runs in Colorado in the form of the Rampart Reservoir Loop and the Barr Trail; they are completely opposite experiences, and yet represent the best in Colorado trail running. The Rampart Reservoir Loop is a 14-mile circuit of Rampart Reservoir, which lies 23 miles west of Colorado Springs. With moderate vertical gain and great views of Pikes Peak and the reservoir, it is perfect for a few hours of peaceful trail cruising. The Barr Trail is an exquisitely maintained torture path featuring vertical gain and more vertical gain - and yet the work does not seem so bad with so many fellow sufferers on the trail. A typical summer weekend will easily see 100 trail runners per day doing mileage on this great trail.

Another trail of note is the Mueller State Park Medley. Though it can be a confusing tangle of trails, one can meet more elk than humans. Solitude and great views make this a worthwhile trail system to explore.

A trail guide is not complete without a good torture trail, and Colorado Springs has a champion - the Cap'n Jack's Trail. With a killer mix of sand, steep uphill, rock gardens, and mad downhill cyclists, this is the perfect workout for those in search of a heart attack.

Barr Trail 44

Descending from Barr Camp.

*T*he is the ultimate Colorado Springs running trail, swarming with dozens of runners on weekends. Be prepared to see upwards of a hundred runners during summer weekends. However, because of the high day-time temperatures on the bottom half of the trail, the parking lot is likely to be full by 6 a.m., so either show up early or be prepared to park further down the road

Location: 6.0 miles west of I-25 in Colorado Springs
Distance/Type: 12.8 miles out and back
Running Time: 1.75 hours on the ascent and 1.25 hours on the descent. The first 3.0 miles are very slow!
Starting Elevation: 6,570 feet
Elevation Gain: 3,530 feet
Best Season: April through October
Jurisdiction: Pike National Forest
Map(s): *Trails Illustrated # 137*
Permits/Fees: None

Grade: The trail has an average ten degree angle of ascent for over six miles, with most of the pain in the first three miles, where the gradient is 14 degrees.

Getting There: Take exit # 141 on I-25 in Colorado Springs and go west on Route 24 for 3.9 miles to the Manitou Springs exit. Turn right off the exit and follow the cog railway signs along Manitou Avenue for 1.3 miles. Then turn left onto Ruxton Avenue and fol-

Rating

Difficult

Classics

Mileage

0.0 Head west out of the parking lot.
2.8 Continue west on the Barr Trail.
3.1 Bear west on the Barr Trail.
6.4 Turn around and retrace path. Head east.
12.8 Arrive back at parking lot.

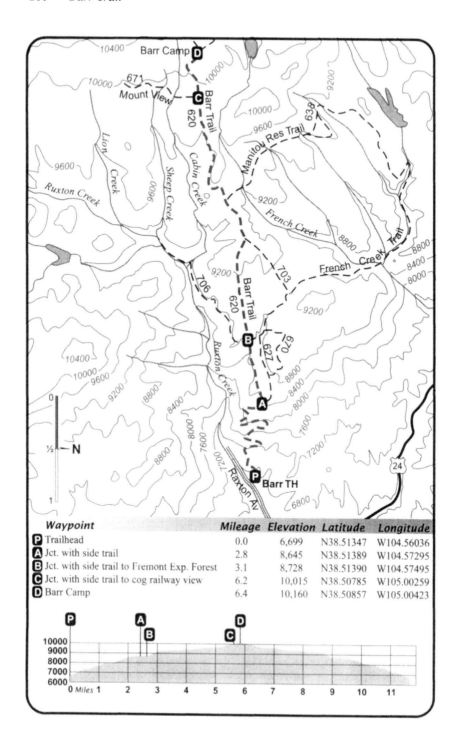

Waypoint	Mileage	Elevation	Latitude	Longitude
P Trailhead	0.0	6,699	N38.51347	W104.56036
A Jct. with side trail	2.8	8,645	N38.51389	W104.57295
B Jct. with side trail to Fremont Exp. Forest	3.1	8,728	N38.51390	W104.57495
C Jct. with side trail to cog railway view	6.2	10,015	N38.50785	W105.00259
D Barr Camp	6.4	10,160	N38.50857	W105.00423

low it past the cog railway station to the end of the road. The parking lot is at the end of a steep uphill spur road to the right at the end of the road. There is a Barr Trail sign pointing the way onto the spur road.

The Route Description

From the parking lot, ascend a short set of stairs and then embark on an interminable series of switchbacks that continue for nearly three miles. There is some gravel on the trail, so traction is a bit suspect at times. Stay left at mile 2.8 (8650), where there is a significant branch trail leading sharply uphill and to the right. Temperatures tend to drop slightly from here on up, as you leave the scorching valley in which the trail begins. Also stay left at mile 3.1 (8730), where another trail leads off to the right to the Old Fremont Experimental Forest. The vegetation changes from the scrub brush of the lower sections to a pleasant pine forest. There is a small side trail to the left at mile 6.2 (10020), leading to a view of the cog railway. Be more careful here, as the trail quality degrades and some rocks, small ledges, and roots put in an appearance. The Barr Camp is located at mile 6.4 (10160). This rustic, fully staffed hut provides water tanks for general use during the summer months. The tanks are located just to the left of its entryway.

Time to turn around and head back, unless you want to brave the final six miles to the summit of Pikes Peak. The descent is excellent, especially in the middle third, where the trail angle is reasonable. Be most careful during the final few miles of the run, since the trail is steeper and there are increasing numbers of hikers, bikers, and runners to avoid. The trailhead will appear at mile 12.8 (6700).

Lounging at Barr Camp.

45 Cap'n Jack's Trail

If you are just starting to run trails or are in poor condition, do not run this route - a number of sections are extremely steep, with loose rocks and gravel. On the other hand, the views are spectacular, especially from the aspen groves in the loop section at the far end of the trail. Also, watch out for dirt bikes and mountain bikes on this increasingly popular trail.

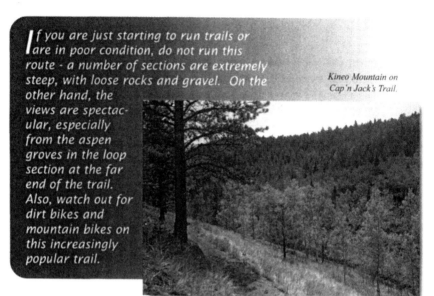

Kineo Mountain on Cap'n Jack's Trail.

Rating

Difficult

Mileage

0.0 Start south on unmarked Cap'n Jack's Trail.
2.1 Go west on Bear Creek Trail.
3.0 Head south on Trail 668.
4.3 Go north on Trail 668.
5.1 Rejoin Bear Creek Trail. Go East.
6.0 Junction with Cap'n Jack's Trail. Head East.
8.1 Arrive back at parking lot.

Location: 8.0 miles west of Colorado Springs
Distance/Type: 8.1 miles out and back
Running Time: 2.0 hours
Starting Elevation: 7,890 feet
Elevation Gain: 2,450 feet
Best Season: April through October
Jurisdiction: Pike National Forest
Map(s): Trails Illustrated # 137
Permits/Fees: None

Grade: A very difficult mix of sand, gravel, and rocks, sometimes including extremely steep ascents and descents. A turned ankle is possible in several sections.

Getting There: Take exit # 141 on I-25 in Colorado Springs and drive 0.3 miles west on Route 24. Turn left onto 8th Street, head south for 1.9 miles, and turn right onto Cheyenne Boulevard. Drive 1.5 miles to the Seven Falls intersection and stay to the right on Cheyenne Boulevard for another 4.7 miles until it splits into several dirt roads. Take the one-way High Drive road north for 1.0 mile, and turn right into the

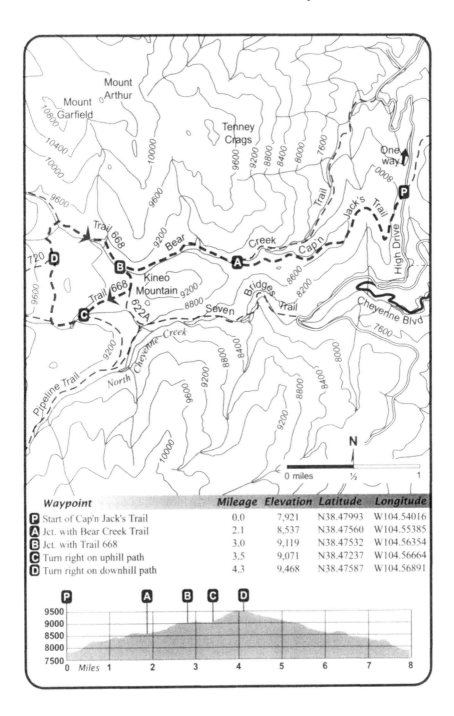

Waypoint	Mileage	Elevation	Latitude	Longitude
P Start of Cap'n Jack's Trail	0.0	7,921	N38.47993	W104.54016
A Jct. with Bear Creek Trail	2.1	8,537	N38.47560	W104.55385
B Jct. with Trail 668	3.0	9,119	N38.47532	W104.56354
C Turn right on uphill path	3.5	9,071	N38.47237	W104.56664
D Turn right on downhill path	4.3	9,468	N38.47587	W104.56891

rough parking area. Please note that, since High Drive is one way, you must continue along the road after you are finished, which merges into 26th Street after several miles. If you follow 26th Street north, it will intersect with Route 24, which leads east to I-25.

The Route Description

From the High Drive road, cross the street and ascend, on a southerly bearing, up the unmarked Cap'n Jack's Trail (there is a sign a short distance down the trail on the left side). The first half-mile is hard, with a non-stop ascent up a loose gravel surface. If you need to pause for breath, check out the views on the left, where there is a valley full of rock pinnacles. At mile 0.5 (7990), the trail reaches a ridgeline, which it follows for 1.5 miles until it drops down into Bear Canyon, linking with the Bear Creek Trail at mile 2.1 (8540) after crossing Bear Creek. Turn left and ascend along the north side of the creek, being very careful not to turn an ankle on the numerous loose rocks. Enter a small aspen grove at mile 3.0 (9120) and turn left, crossing Bear Creek to access trail number 668. If you are a true glutton for punishment, you can turn right here instead and continue up the valley for several more miles. Follow trail 668 until mile 3.5 (9070), where the trail splits. Turn right at this fork and run up a brutally steep hill, which eventually levels out in a beautiful aspen grove. This is a good time for a break. Then continue uphill at a more modest angle until mile 4.3 (9470), where you take a right turn onto a narrower trail that drops rapidly through an aspen grove and then descends very steeply until it returns you to Bear Creek at mile 5.1 (9120). Cross the creek and turn right to follow the Bear Creek Trail back down along Bear Creek to mile 6.0 (9120), where you leave the trail, turning right to cross the creek once more and ascend up to the ridge line on the Cap'n Jack's Trail. The return trip on Cap'n Jack's is much easier than the outbound run. Cruise back down the trail until you reach the parking lot at mile 8.1 (7920).

Lovell Gulch Loop 46

North end of the Lovell Gulch Trail

*T*his is the perfect weekend run because it has very little traffic, which seems to crowd nearby Rampart Reservoir. Additionally, this route offers great views of Pikes Peak and Ute Pass.

Rating

Moderate

Location: 19.0 miles west of Colorado Springs
Distance/Type: 5.5 miles loop
Running Time: 1.25 hours
Starting Elevation: 8,640 feet
Elevation Gain: 1,150 feet
Best Season: April through October
Jurisdiction: Pike National Forest
Map(s): *Trails Illustrated # 137*
Permits/Fees: None

Grade: Moderate, except for a root-filled section just prior to the high point. Also, watch out for a steep descent from the high point over loose gravel.

Getting There: From Exit #141 on I-25 in Colorado Springs, turn west onto Route 24 and proceed 16.9 miles to Baldwin Street. Take a right on that street and continue past a school on the right and another on the left, for 2.2 miles. Turn left into a parking just prior to a government facility with a water tank.

GO

Mileage

0.0 Head west on Lovell Gulch Trail.
0.1 Turn north on Lovell Gulch Trail.
0.8 Go east on Lovell Gulch Trail.
2.3 Turn west on Lovell Gulch Trail.
4.7 Head south on Lovell Gulch Trail.
5.5 Arrive back at parking lot.

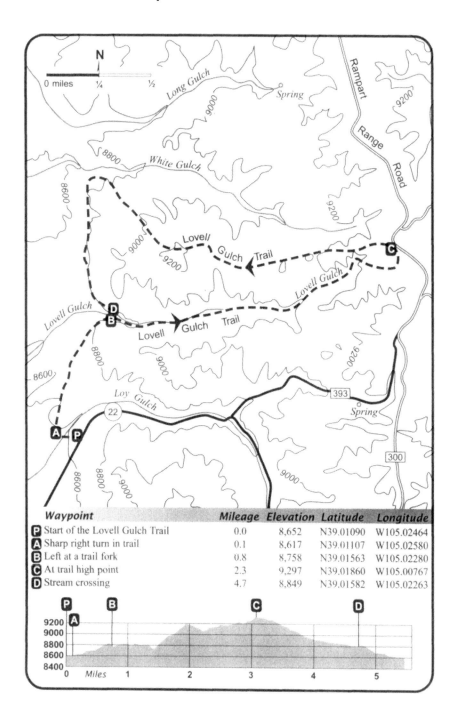

Waypoint	Mileage	Elevation	Latitude	Longitude
P Start of the Lovell Gulch Trail	0.0	8,652	N39.01090	W105.02464
A Sharp right turn in trail	0.1	8,617	N39.01107	W105.02580
B Left at a trail fork	0.8	8,758	N39.01563	W105.02280
C At trail high point	2.3	9,297	N39.01860	W105.00767
D Stream crossing	4.7	8,849	N39.01582	W105.02263

A view of Pikes Peak along the Lovell Gulch Trail.

The Route Description

Open the gate at the end of the parking lot and drop slightly downhill along a double track trail. The trail bends sharply to the right at mile 0.1 (8620). Ignore a trail on the left at this junction and jog gradually uphill through open stands of pine trees. At mile 0.8 (8760), turn left at a fork in the trail, dropping abruptly and crossing a small stream. Immediately thereafter, you will see the Lovell Gulch Trail, for which there is a sign. Turn right onto this trail. Though you can turn left to run the route in reverse, it is a much more difficult ascent to the high point. Continue up through pine forests as the trail becomes increasingly root-infested. At mile 2.3 (9300), you are now at the high point of the route; there is a junction with a road, overhead power lines, and a locked gate. Turn left past the gate and follow the trail downhill beneath the power lines, passing over several short, steep ascents. At mile 3.5, you will come to a point on the double track trail where an obvious single track trail branches to the right. Stay left on the double track trail and drop precipitously down a steep gravel slope. The trail will switch back sharply to the right and then gradually curve back left as it loses altitude. At mile 4.7 (8850), arrive back at the junction by the stream. Turn right at the Lovell Gulch Trail sign and cross the stream again. From there, follow the trail as it winds gently back to the trailhead, which you will find at mile 5.5 (8650).

47 Mueller State Park Medley

Though the views are pleasant enough, the trail system is confusing - there are many short, interlocking trails, all of which are identified with trail numbers rather than names. Accordingly, it is quite easy to become lost here. Though much longer runs can be derived from the park's trail system, I have only included a short medley of trails that can be followed in a clockwise manner in order to avoid confusion. Bring a map when you run in this park! Also, portions of the park will be closed during June for elk calving, so call ahead to find out which trails are open.

Pikes Peak from Trail # 25.

Rating

Easy

Mileage **GO**

0.0 Start west out of parking lot.
0.1 Head west and south on Trail 11.
0.8 Continue of Trail 25. Head north.
2.1 Turn east on Trail 13.
2.3 Go south on Trail 12.
3.4 Turn south on Trail 1.
3.9 Arrive back at parking lot.

Location: 29.0 miles west of Colorado Springs
Distance/Type: 3.9 miles medley
Running Time: 45 minutes
Starting Elevation: 9,670 feet
Elevation Gain: 650 feet
Best Season: May through October
Jurisdiction: Mueller State Park and Wildlife Area
Map(s): Trails Illustrated # 137
Permits/Fees: $5 park fee

Grade: Easy, though there are a series of short hill climbs on loose gravel

Getting There: From Exit #141 on I-25 in Colorado Springs, drive west on Route 24 for 24.3 miles to the town of Divide. Turn left on southbound Route 67, and follow it 3.7 miles to the Mueller State Park turnoff on the right side of the road. After paying the park fee at the gate, drive 1.8 miles to the Lost Pond Trailhead, which will be on the left.

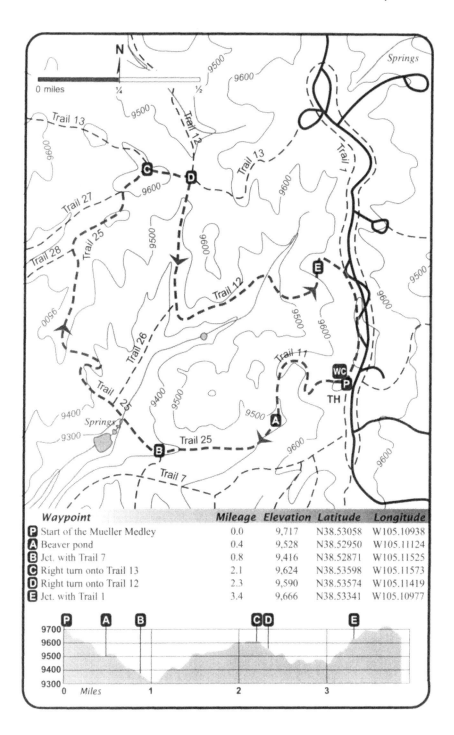

Waypoint	Mileage	Elevation	Latitude	Longitude
P Start of the Mueller Medley	0.0	9,717	N38.53058	W105.10938
A Beaver pond	0.4	9,528	N38.52950	W105.11124
B Jct. with Trail 7	0.8	9,416	N38.52871	W105.11525
C Right turn onto Trail 13	2.1	9,624	N38.53598	W105.11573
D Right turn onto Trail 12	2.3	9,590	N38.53574	W105.11419
E Jct. with Trail 1	3.4	9,666	N38.53341	W105.10977

The beaver pond at mile 0.4.

The Route Description

From the trailhead, follow a short trail for 0.1 miles to a three-way junction with Trail 1. Turn right here and then turn left onto Trail 11, which takes you downhill to a beaver pond at mile 0.40 (9530). The trail designation changes to Trail 25 at this point. Continue down the wide and gravelly path to mile 0.8 (9420), which is a junction with Trail 7. Ignore Trail 7 and continue on Trail 25 as it heads north past Geer Pond and through a series of short, steep hills and stands of aspen trees. At mile 2.1 (9620), turn right onto Trail 13. At mile 2.3, turn right onto Trail 12 (9590). However, if you wish to explore the northern portions of the park, this is a good place to turn left instead - just make sure you have a map! At mile 2.7, there will be a junction with Trail 26. Stay left to avoid Trail 26 and stay on Trail 12. At mile 3.4 (9670), arrive at a four-way junction with Trail 1, which travels in a north-south direction and parallels the main park road. Turn right onto this trail and run south to the sign indicating a left turn back to the parking area. Huff up the short access trail to the parking lot, located at mile 3.9 (9720).

Rampart Reservoir Loop 48

*T*his is one of the great trail runs in Colorado, with fabulous views of Pikes Peak and easy running conditions. However, it is a busy trail on the weekends, but more so within the first two miles of the trailhead. The far side of the reservoir is relatively quiet. When in doubt about the correct trail to choose, always stay close to the shoreline.

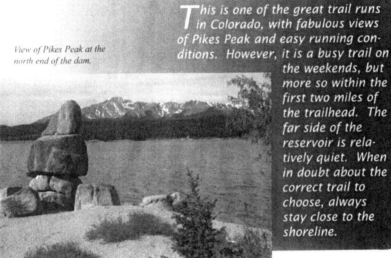

View of Pikes Peak at the north end of the dam.

Rating

Difficult

Classics

Location: 23.0 miles west of Colorado Springs
Distance/Type: 4.3 miles loop
Running Time: 3.0 hours
Starting Elevation: 9,280 feet
Elevation Gain: 1,500 feet
Best Season: May through October
Jurisdiction: Pike National Forest
Map(s): *Trails Illustrated # 48*
Permits/Fees: None

Grade: Easy, with rolling hills. There are numerous gravel sections.

Getting There: From Exit # 141 on I-25 in Colorado Springs, turn west onto Route 24 and proceed 16.9 miles to Baldwin Street. Take a right on that street and continue past a school on the right and another on the left for 2.8 miles. Turn right onto Loy Creek Road. Continue for 1.5 miles and then turn right onto the Rampart Range Road. Travel for another 2.3 miles to the Rainbow Gulch Trailhead, which is on the left side of the road. Park here.

GO

Mileage
0.0 Start east out of the parking lot.
1.3 Continue east on the south side of the reservoir.
5.6 The rampart trail starts heading west.
13.0 Turn west on Rampart Trail. Head towards the parking lot.
14.3 Arrive back at parking lot.

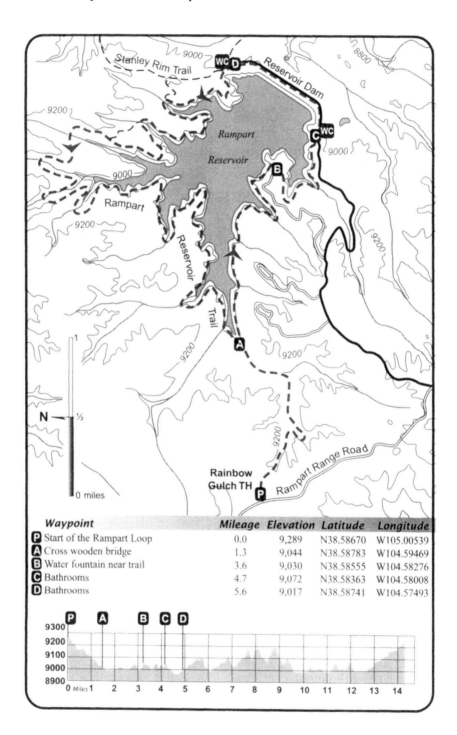

Waypoint	Mileage	Elevation	Latitude	Longitude
P Start of the Rampart Loop	0.0	9,289	N38.58670	W105.00539
A Cross wooden bridge	1.3	9,044	N38.58783	W104.59469
B Water fountain near trail	3.6	9,030	N38.58555	W104.58276
C Bathrooms	4.7	9,072	N38.58363	W104.58008
D Bathrooms	5.6	9,017	N38.58741	W104.57493

The Route Description

Run downhill along a winding dirt road for 0.75 mile to where a stream emerges from an underground culvert. The road splits here, with a double track version continuing down the left side of the stream, and a more pleasant single track version going down the right side (though swarming with fishermen). Take your pick of trails, since they merge further downstream.

If you took the trail on the left, it is time to cross a wooden bridge at mile 1.3 (9040) to rejoin the single track version of the trail. Then follow the trail towards the reservoir. The trail will fade slightly as it turns toward the right. Follow it for a few hundred yards as it curls back inland and meets the main reservoir trail. Turn left onto this trail and follow it along the shoreline. From this point onward, when in doubt, always take the choice of trail nearest the shoreline. There is a water fountain next to the trail at mile 3.6 (9030), and there are two picnic platforms nearby. You will continue around the edge of multiple inlets. Ahead, watch for the dam at the east end of the reservoir as you gradually approach it.

There is a set of bathrooms at mile 4.7 (9070) next to a paved parking lot at the south end of the dam. Continue along the trail to the left of the bathrooms, which will bring you to the dam road. Turn left onto the road and run across the dam (sorry, it's paved, but it's only for 0.8 miles!). There is yet another bathroom at mile 5.6 (9020) on the far side of the dam. The trail continues straight ahead and then turns sharply left to hug the shoreline on its way down the far side of the reservoir. Be sure to stop at mile 6.0 (9010), where there is a three-tiered stack of rocks overlooking Pikes Peak to the south.

At mile 7.9 (9090) the trail diverges from the shoreline, heading inland about 150 yards, at which point it turns back to the shore. Continue down the shoreline, dipping in and out of a series of delightful inlets. The trail gradually finishes circling the reservoir, bringing you back to the bridge crossing. Take your pick of which side of the stream to follow, and run uphill along it back to the parking lot, located at mile 14.3 (9290).

49 Stratton Medley

A pleasant local run through local scrub brush and a few pine trees. The main problem is the plethora of trails jammed into a relatively small park. It is useful to bring this guide and a GPS unit the first time you run the recommended loop in order to get a feel for the park. After that, try any of the many unmarked trails that wander through the park.

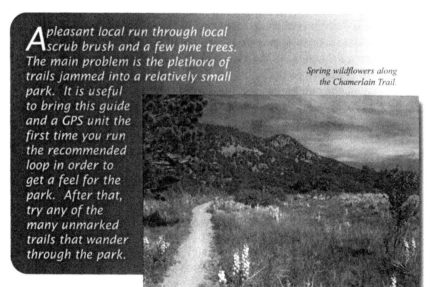

Spring wildflowers along the Chamerlain Trail.

Rating

Moderate

Go

Mileage

0.0 Start west out of parking lot.
0.5 Bear south and east on Chamberlain Trail.
1.9 Go north on Upper Meadows Loop.
2.7 Head southwest on Ponderosa Trail.
3.5 Head northwest on Chutes Trail.
4.3 Retrace route down Chutes Trail.
5.4 Turn west then north on Chamberlain Trail.
5.9 Arrive at parking lot.

Location: 3.0 miles west of Colorado Springs
Distance/Type: 5.9 miles medley
Running Time: 1.25 hours
Starting Elevation: 6,315 feet
Elevation Gain: 1,120 feet
Best Season: March through November
Jurisdiction: Pike National Forest
Map(s): *Trails Illustrated # 137*
Permits/Fees: None

Grade: Intermediate. Easy double track and single track, with a few moderately strenuous sections. Some portions of the trail are deeply rutted.

Getting There: Take exit # 141 on I-25 in Colorado Springs and drive 0.3 miles west on Route 24. Turn left onto 8th Street, head south for 1.9 miles, and turn right onto Cheyenne Boulevard. Drive 1.5 miles to the Seven Falls intersection and stay to the right on Cheyenne Boulevard for another 0.3 miles. Stop in the parking area for the Stratton Open Space on the right side of the road.

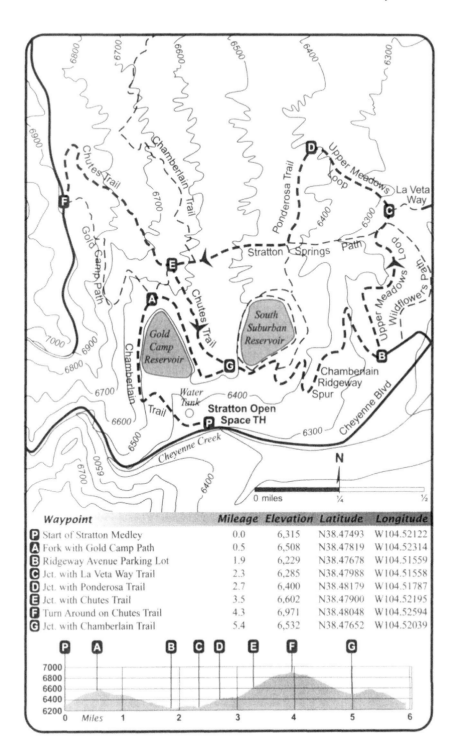

Waypoint	Mileage	Elevation	Latitude	Longitude
P Start of Stratton Medley	0.0	6,315	N38.47493	W104.52122
A Fork with Gold Camp Path	0.5	6,508	N38.47819	W104.52314
B Ridgeway Avenue Parking Lot	1.9	6,229	N38.47678	W104.51559
C Jct. with La Veta Way Trail	2.3	6,285	N38.47988	W104.51558
D Jct. with Ponderosa Trail	2.7	6,400	N38.48179	W104.51787
E Jct. with Chutes Trail	3.5	6,602	N38.47900	W104.52195
F Turn Around on Chutes Trail	4.3	6,971	N38.48048	W104.52594
G Jct. with Chamberlain Trail	5.4	6,532	N38.47652	W104.52039

The Route Description

Take the trail at the west end of the parking lot, which is the Chamberlain Trail. Stay to the left of a large water tower and take the middle of three double track trails, which is clearly marked. Continue uphill over a sandy grade to the west side of the Gold Camp Reservoir. The trail shrinks to single track at 0.3 miles (6515) as it follows along the west side of the reservoir to the left of a chain link fence. The trail loops around the north side of the reservoir, passing the Gold Camp Path at 0.5 miles (6580). Stay on the Chamberlain Trail as it turns east, southeast, and then due east as it heads toward the South Suburban Reservoir, which you will reach after 1.0 miles (6490). From here, take the unmarked Chamberlain-Ridgeway Spur, which is a wide, well-graded dirt road that passes to the southeast of the reservoir and gradually loops through several switchbacks until it reaches the parking lot at Ridgeway Avenue at 1.9 miles (6250). Just before reaching the parking lot, turn left onto the Upper Meadows Loop, which is a single track trail that gradually ascends along the east side of the park. At mile 2.3 (6250), turn left to stay on the Upper Meadows Loop. If you go straight here, you will end up at the La Veta Way parking lot. At mile 2.7 (6400), turn left onto the Ponderosa Trail. At mile 2.8 (6450), turn right onto the Upper Meadows Loop. This is the start of the best running in the park, with more pine trees and shade. At mile 3.5 (6590), turn right onto the Chutes Trail. Turn right again at mile 3.6 (6610) to stay on the Chutes Trail, which ascends along a sandy and deeply rutted trail into the northwestern corner of the park. Reach the turnaround point at mile 4.3 (6970), which intersects with a local road. It is also possible to continue down the Gold Camp Path Trail to the starting point, though this is a somewhat steeper and rockier trail than the Chutes Trail. Run back down the Chutes Trail and stay on it until you reach a junction with the Chamberlain Trail at mile 5.4 (6,530). Turn right to stay on the Chamberlain Trail and follow it back around the Gold Camp Reservoir and to the parking lot, located at mile 5.9 (6320).

Waldo Canyon Loop 50

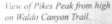
View of Pikes Peak from high on Waldo Canyon Trail.

With **its beautiful views of Waldo Canyon, this is a very popular run, and therefore, is very busy. Be sure to come early, and be careful to go slow to avoid tripping over roots and other sharp rocks.**

Rating

Moderate

Location: 7.0 miles west of I-25, near Colorado Springs.

Distance/Type: 6.9 miles loop

Running Time: 1.5 hours

Starting Elevation: 7,050 feet

Elevation Gain: 2,000 feet

Best Season: April through October

Jurisdiction: Pike National Forest

Map(s): *Trails Illustrated # 137*

Permits/Fees: None

Grade: Moderate, with many tight switchbacks. There are a number of roots and snags, as well as sandy sections. Nonetheless, most portions of the trail are in good condition.

Getting There: From Exit # 141 in Colorado Springs, take Route 24 west for 7.4 miles and turn right into the large Waldo Canyon parking area.

Mileage *GO*

0.0 Head west out of parking lot.

0.4 Continue north on the trail.

1.7 Go south on Waldo Canyon Trail.

4.3 Turn south on Waldo Canyon Trail.

5.2 Turn southwest on trail.

6.9 Arrive back at parking lot.

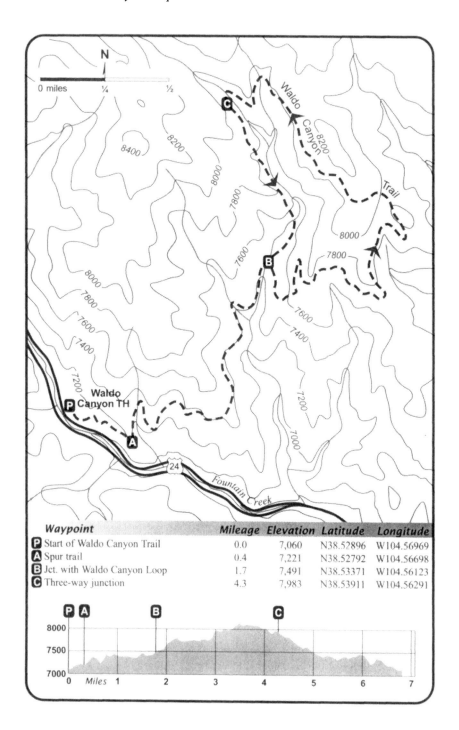

Waypoint	Mileage	Elevation	Latitude	Longitude
P Start of Waldo Canyon Trail	0.0	7,060	N38.52896	W104.56969
A Spur trail	0.4	7,221	N38.52792	W104.56698
B Jct. with Waldo Canyon Loop	1.7	7,491	N38.53371	W104.56123
C Three-way junction	4.3	7,983	N38.53911	W104.56291

The Route Description

From the parking lot, walk up a set of stairs and then begin running up a gentle incline on a good trail surface. At mile 0.4 (7220), there is a spur trail branching to the right, giving a good overlook of the highway. The trail continues to the left. At mile 1.7 (7490), you have arrived at the Waldo Canyon Loop Trail. Turn right at the sign. The trail becomes sandy in places and can provide slippery footing as you ascend through a series of tight switchbacks, crossing an open ridge at 7,750 feet and then turning north to reach the high point of the run at 8,150 feet. The trail then gradually descends to the northwest. There is a three-way junction at mile 4.3 (7980), where you should turn hard left down a short stair case to continue on your way. A sign indicates the proper path. Arrive back at the beginning of the loop trail at mile 5.2 (7490). Watch out for uphill traffic as you motor down the easy cruising trail to the parking lot at mile 6.9 (7060).

Appendix

*Along the Meyers
Homestead Trail.*

Land Management Agencies

Boulder Parks and Recreation
3198 Broadway
Boulder, CO 80304
303-413-7200

Boulder City Open Space and Mountain Parks
PO Box 791
Boulder, CO 80436
303-441-3440
www.osmp.org

Castlewood Canyon State Park
Box 504
Franktown, CO 80116
303-688-5242

Colorado Springs Parks and Recreation
1401 Recreation Way
Colorado Springs, CO 80905
719-385-5940

Colorado State Parks
1313 Sherman St. # 618
Denver, CO 80203
303-866-3437
www.parks.state.co.us

Douglas County Parks and Trails Division
9651 South Quebec
Highlands Ranch, CO 80126
303-470-0140

Denver Mountain Parks
300 Union
Morrison, CO 80465
303-697-4545
www.Denvergov.org

Golden Gate Canyon State Park
3873 Highway 46
Golden, CO 80403
303-582-3707

Jefferson County Open Space
700 Jefferson Cty. Pkwy, Ste. 100
Golden, CO 80401

Lakewood Regional Parks
480 S. Allison Pkwy.
Lakewood, CO 80206
303-987-7000
www.lakewood.org

Mueller State Park
P.O. Box 39
Divide, CO 80814

Pike National Forest
Pikes Peak Ranger District
601 South Weber
Colorado Springs, CO 80461
719-636-1602

South Platte District
19316 Goddard Ranch Court
Morrison, CO 80465
303-697-0414

Roosevelt National Forest
Boulder Ranger District
2140 Yarmouth Avenue
Boulder, CO 80301
303-444-6600
www.fs.fed.us/r2/arnf/

Roxborough State Park
4751 N. Roxborough Drive
Littleton, CO 80125
(303) 973-3959

Trail Races in Colorado

January
Colorado Governor's Cup
(5K)
Frisco, CO
303-635-2815
www.emgcolorado.com

Off Track, Off Beat Snowshoe
Race
(10K)
Leadville, CO
719-486-3581
www.racingunderground.com

Turquoise Lake Snowshoe
(20 miles)
Leadville, CO
719-486-3581
www.racingunderground.com

February
Devils Thumb Adventure Race
(30K)
Frasier, CO
303-635-2815
www.emgcolorado.com

Frisco Gold Rush
(5K)
Frisco, CO
303-635-2815
www.emgcolorado.com

High Altitude Snowshoe Race
(5K, 10K)
Silverton, CO
970-387-5522
www.ci.silverton.co.us

February
The Screamin' Snowman
(5K, 10K)
Eldora, CO
(303)527-1798
www.racingunderground.com

March
America's Uphill
(2.7 miles)
Aspen, CO
970-925-9360
www.utemountaineer.com

April
Snowshoe Shuffle in Beaver Creek
(5K, 10K)
Avon, CO
970-926-7485
www.vvmc.com

Collegiate Peaks Races
(25 & 50 miles)
Buena Vista, CO
719-395-6612
www.fourteenernet.com/buenavista

Lory Trail Run
(9.5 miles)
Fort Collins, CO
970-221-0080
www.runnersroostftcollins.com

Panoramic Run
(4 miles)
Colorado Springs, CO
719-598-2953
www.pprun.org

May
Spirit Challenge
(5K, 10K)
Steamboat Springs, CO
970-879-4234
www.runningseries.com

June
Aspen Grove Trail Race
(6.2 mi., 13.1 mi., 26.2 mi.)
Aspen, CO
303-929-8681
www.exploreadventures.com

Horsetooth Mountain Trail Run
(8.5 miles)
Fort Collins, CO
970-224-9114
www.runnersroostftcollins.com

Mount Evans Ascent
(14 miles)
Evergreen, CO
970-389-4838
www.racingunderground.com

Spring Creek Memorial
(5K, 10K)
Steamboat Springs, CO
970-879-6342
www.runningseries.com

Spring Run Off
(6.5 miles)
Vail, CO
970-479-2280
www.vailrec.com

July
Barr Trail Mountain Race
(12 miles)
Manitou Springs, CO
719-685-5654
www.runpikespeak.com

Firecracker Trail Run
(5K, 10K)
Colorado Springs, CO
719-635-8803
www.csgrandprix.com

Hardrock 100
(100 miles)
Silverton, CO
970-259-3693
www.run100s.com

Leadville Trail Marathon
(26.2 miles)
Leadville, CO
719-486-3502
www.leadvilletrail100.com

Oh My God Run
(8 miles)
Idaho Springs, CO
303-871-8366
www.rmrr.org

Run for Independence
(5 miles)
Winter Park, CO
800-903-7275
www.winterpark-info.com

Vail Hill Climb
(7.5 miles)
Vail, CO
970-479-2280
www.vailrec.com

August
Aspen Mountain Uphill
(4.4 miles)
Aspen, CO
970-927-0265
clkeleher@hotmail.com

Berry Picker Trail Hill Climb
(3 miles)
Vail, CO
970-479-2280
www.vailrec.com

Breckenridge Crest Mountain
Marathon
(5 miles, 10 miles, 24.5 miles)
Breckenridge, CO
970-453-6422
www.breckenridgesports.com

Continental Divide Trail Run
(15 miles)
Steamboat Springs, CO
970-879-0385
www.runningseries.com

Leadville Trail 100
(100 miles)
Leadville, CO
719-486-3502
www.leadvilletrail100.com

Mount Werner Classic
(5 miles, 12 miles)
Steamboat Springs, CO
970-870-1975
www.runningseries.com

Pikes Peak Ascent
(13.4 miles)
Manitou Springs, CO
719-473-2625

Pikes Peak Marathon
(26.2 miles)
Manitou Springs, CO
719-473-2625
www.pikespeakmarathon.org

UCCS Stampede Cross Country
(5K)
Colorado Springs, CO
www.pprun.org

September
America Discovery Trail Marathon
(26.2 miles)
Colorado Springs, CO
719-635-3833
www.adtmarathon.com

Autumn Color Run
(13.1 miles)
Buena Vista, CO
719-395-6612
www.fourteenernet.com

Bacon Strip Trail Races
(4 miles, 10 miles)
Fort Collins, CO
970-224-9114
www.runnersroostftcollins.com

Boulder Backroads Marathon
(13.1 miles and 26.2 miles)
Boulder, CO
303-939-9661
www.boulderbackroads.com

Breckenridge Crest Mountain
Marathon
(5 miles, 10 miles, 24.5 miles)
Breckenridge, CO
970-453-6422
www.boec.org

Golden Leaf Half Marathon
(13.5 miles)
Aspen, CO
970-925-9360
www.utemountaineer.com

Imogene Pass Run
(17.1 miles)
Ouray, CO
970-255-1002
www.csbservices.com

Kokopelli Adventure Race
(2 days)
Grand Junction, CO
303-635-2815
www.emgcolorado.com

Roadkill Trail Half Marathon
(13.1 miles)
Kremmling, CO
970-724-3472
www.kremmlingchamber.com

October
Fall Cross Country Series
(3.5 miles)
Colorado Springs, CO
719-590-7086
www.pprrun.org

Fall Cross Country Series
(6 miles)
Colorado Springs, CO
719-590-7086
www.pprrun.org

Telegraph Trail
(25K, 50K)
Durango, CO
970-375-2413
www.durangomarathon.com

November
Beaver Creek Snowshoe Fun Fest
(10K)
970-476-6797
www.bcsnowshoe.com

Fall Cross Country Series
(7.5 miles)
Colorado Springs, CO
719-590-7086
www.pprrun.org

Off Track, Off Beat Snowshoe
Race
(10K)
Leadville, CO
719-486-3581
www.racingunderground.com

Salomon Winter Adventure Series
Snowshoe
(5K)
Winter Park, CO
303-635-2815
www.emgcolorado.com

December
Beaver Creek Snowshoe Fun Fest
(10K)
Beaver Creek, CO
970-476-6797
www.bcsnowshoe.com

Index

THE COLORADO MOUNTAIN CLUB

The Colorado Mountain Club is a non-profit outdoor recreation, education and conservation organization founded in 1912. Today with over 10,000 members, 14 branches in-state, and one branch for out-of-state members, the CMC is the largest organization of its kind in the Rocky Mountains. *Membership opens the door to:*

Outdoor Recreation: *Over 3100 trips and outings led annually.* Hike, ski, climb, backpack, snowshoe, bicycle, ice skate, travel the world and build friendships that will last a lifetime.

Conservation: *Supporting a mission which treasures our natural environment.* Committed to environmental education, a strong voice on public lands management, trail building and rehabilitation projects.

Outdoor Education: *Schools, seminars, and courses that teach outdoor skills through hands-on activities.* Wilderness trekking, rock climbing, high altitude mountaineering, telemark skiing, backpacking and much more — plus our Youth Education Program *(YEP!)* designed to inspire lifelong stewardship in children and young adults.

Publications: *A wide range of outdoor publications to benefit and inform members.* Trail and Timberline Magazine, twice-a-year Activity Schedule, monthly group newsletters, and 20% discount on titles from CMC Press.

The American Mountaineering Center: *A world-class facility in Golden, Colorado.* Featuring the largest mountaineering library in the western hemisphere, a mountaineering museum, a 300-seat, state-of-the-art auditorium, a conference center, free monthly program nights and a climbing wall.

Visit the beautiful American Mountaineering Center!

JOINING IS EASY!

Membership opens the door to:
ADVENTURE!

The Colorado Mountain Club
710 10th St. #200 Golden, CO 80401
(303) 279-3080 1(800) 633-4417
FAX (303) 279-9690
Email: cmcoffice@cmc.org
Website: www.cmc.org

MEMBERSHIP OPENS THE DOOR . . .

CAMPING TREKKING ROCK CLIMBING SCHOOLS MOUNTAINEERING

NEW RELEASE   FALL 2004!

THE TRAD GUIDE TO JOSHUA TREE: 60 Favorite Climbs from 5.5 to 5.9 *by Charlie and Diane Winger* Many climbers who visit Joshua Tree spend as much time searching for good routes as they do actually climbing. This guidebook offers the moderate climber a fun, varied and challenging "tick-list" of 60 great *Trad* climbs, and makes it easy to find your way around. With color photos of every route, detailed maps, and easy-to-follow driving and hiking directions, you'll be able to climb numerous routes per day and make the most of your climbing trip.

More Colorado titles for you to enjoy from the Colorado Mountain Club Press:

GUIDE TO THE COLORADO MOUNTAINS, 10th Edition, *edited by Randy Jacobs.* The complete guide to Colorado's peaks, passes, lakes and trails is more complete than ever with over 1,500 hiking and climbing destinations and a ranked listing of the state's 200 highest summits. The best-selling Colorado book of all time, with nearly 1/4 million in print.

THE COLORADO TRAIL: THE OFFICIAL GUIDEBOOK, 6th Edition, *by The Colorado Trail Foundation.* Written for both through hikers or those doing a section at a time, this comprehensive guide has everything you need: detailed descriptions of every mile, resupply information, natural history, color maps and elevation profiles, and over 90 full-color photos. New features include over 800 GPS locations, plus *Gudy's Tips!*

COLORADO SUMMIT HIKES FOR EVERYONE, *by Dave Muller.* Expertly described routes to 105 classic Colorado summits, complete with full-color maps, elevation profiles and photos for novice to expert level.

THE ANNUAL OFFICIAL COLORADO MOUNTAIN CLUB SCENIC CALENDAR: THE FOURTEENERS. This large, full-color wall calendar captures gorgeous images of the CMC's favorite peaks from CMC members and award-winning photographer Todd Caudle — *an annual favorite!*

COLORADO!
It's Your Place

Explore it with books from the experts in the Rockies
The Colorado Mountain Club Press   www.cmc.org

CPSIA information can be obtained at www.ICGtesting.com
Printed in the USA
241977LV00004B/1/P

9 780972 441353